Ecuador

Ecuador

BY MARION MORRISON

Enchantment of the World
Second Series

Children's Press®

A Division of Grolier Publishing

NEW YORK   LONDON   HONG KONG   SYDNEY
DANBURY, CONNECTICUT

Frontispiece: Guards in nineteenth-century uniform outside the presidential palace

Consultant: Louis R. Sadler, Ph.D., is a Latin American historian and the Department Head of History at New Mexico State University.

Please note: All statistics are as up-to-date as possible at the time of publication.

Visit Children's Press on the Internet: http://publishing.grolier.com

Book Production by Herman Adler Design Group

Library of Congress Cataloging-in-Publication Data

Morrison, Marion
    Ecuador / by Marion Morrison.
      p. cm. — (Enchantment of the world. Second series)
    Includes bibliographical references and index.
    Summary: Describes the geography, history, economy, natural resources, culture, religion, and people of the South American country of Ecuador.
    ISBN 0-516-21544-2
    1. Ecuador—Juvenile literature. [1. Ecuador.] I. Title. II. Series.
F3708.5.M67 2000
986.6—dc21   99-045489

Acknowledgments

Marion Morrison wishes to thank the following people and organizations for their help in the preparation of this book. In Ecuador, Fundación Natura and the Catholic University of Ecuador, Quito; the Municipalities of Otavalo and Quevedo; and the staff of the Chamber of Commerce, Guayaquil. In London, Sra. Nydia Casey and the Embassy of Ecuador; and the staff and libraries at Canning House and the Royal Geographical Society.

Contents

Cover photo:
Indian women outside
a church in Cuenca

Cotopaxi Volcano

A Valdivia Venus

The Middle of the World

A FEW MILES NORTH OF QUITO, ECUADOR'S CAPITAL, stands the *Mitad del Mundo* (Middle of the World) monument. It is a 98-foot (30-meter)-high block of stone, topped by a metal globe. On the ground in front of it, a 4-inch (10-centimeter)-wide strip of white pebbles marks the imaginary line of the Earth's equator. Straddle the line, and you are standing in the Northern and Southern Hemispheres at the same time.

Opposite: **The city of Quito is Ecuador's capital.**

This avenue of statues leads to the Middle of the World Monument.

The monument not only marks the equator, it also commemorates the 1736 expedition that established the exact position of the equator. The expedition was led by French scientist Charles-Marie de La Condamine, and its main task was to determine the shape of the Earth. Was it a globe flattened at the poles, as Isaac Newton maintained, or was the Earth lengthened at the poles and pulled in at the equator, as the French scientists thought? La Condamine proved Newton's case. At the same time, the expedition determined the unit of measurement that resulted in the metric system.

Leading downhill from the monument, an avenue is lined with statues of members of La Condamine's expedition. Among them is an Ecuadorian named Pedro Vicente Maldonado y Sotomayor. Maldonado was a remarkable man—a scientist, a mathematician, an explorer, and a cartographer. He spoke Spanish and French fluently, as well as the native language Quichua. His knowledge of the Andes Mountains, the Amazon jungles, and the coast was unequaled at the time.

Maldonado made one of the most complete maps of the Audiencia of Quito, as Ecuador was then called, and he accompanied La Condamine on the first scientific journey down the mighty Amazon River in 1743. Maldonado was elected a member of the Academy of Sciences in Paris and the Royal Society in London as well as every other brilliant scientific society in Europe. He died at age forty in London of measles.

Another statue is that of Jean Godin des Odonais of France. At the age of thirty, he fell in love with and married a

beautiful thirteen-year-old Ecuadorian girl called Isabella, who came from the southern town of Cuenca. When the expedition's scientific work came to an end, Godin decided to take her back to Europe—by way of the Amazon. To acquaint himself with the dangers and make all necessary arrangements, he first made the extraordinary journey by himself. The horrendous 3,000-mile (4,828-kilometer) trip took four months. He planned to return for his wife by way of the Amazon with help from either the French or Portuguese government.

**Geopolitical map
of Ecuador**

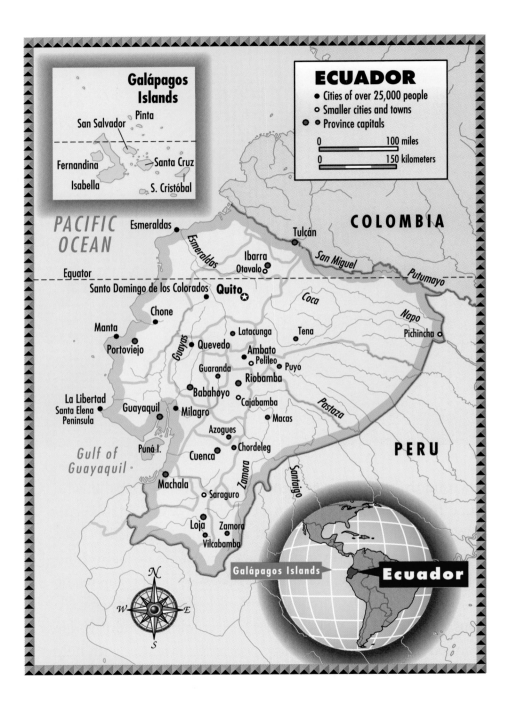

Galápagos
Islands

Pinta
San Salvador

Fernandina

Santa Cruz

Isabella

S. Cristóbal

ECUADOR
- Cities of over 25,000 people
- Smaller cities and towns
- Province capitals

0   100 miles

0   150 kilometers

PACIFIC
OCEAN

Esmeraldas

Tulcán

COLOMBIA

San Miguel

Equator

Ibarra
Otavalo

Putumayo

Santo Domingo de los Colorados

Quito

Coca

Chone

Napo

Manta

Latacunga

Tena

Pichincha

Portoviejo

Quevedo

Ambato
Pelileo

Puyo

Guaranda

Riobamba

Babahoyo

Cajabamba

La Libertad
Santa Elena
Peninsula

Guayaquil

Milagro

Macas

Pastaza

Azogues

Gulf of
Guayaquil

Puná I.

Chordeleg

Cuenca

PERU

Machala

Saraguro

Loja

Zamora

Vilcabamba

N

W   E

S

Galápagos Islands

Ecuador

However, after a great deal of intrigue and many misunderstandings, more than twenty years passed before Godin was able to get word to his wife that a boat was on its way to get her. Madame Isabella Godin had spent those long years in her Andean home waiting patiently for news of her husband and, during that time, their four children had died of various tropical diseases.

In 1769, the fearless Madame Godin set out on the journey with her twelve-year-old nephew, two brothers, three servants, three Frenchmen who were strangers to her, a black man named Joachim, and some Andean Indians. They did not get far before disaster struck. Smallpox, river rapids, fear, the desertion of the Indians, and deception by one of the Frenchmen left only Madame Godin and Joachim. She too was presumed dead—and indeed, she almost was. Separated from Joachim, she wandered alone in the jungle for nine days before she was found by some kind Indians. She later said that only the thought of seeing her husband again inspired her to go on. Reunited with the ever-faithful Joachim, Isabella Godin sailed 2,000 miles (3,218 km) down the Amazon to the Atlantic Ocean and then on to Cayenne in French Guiana, where her husband was waiting. The couple traveled together to France in 1773 with Joachim, thirty-eight years after Jean Godin had left that country.

The success of the French expedition had a further impact on Ecuador. The word *equator—ecuador* in Spanish—was the name given to the new republic when it achieved independence from Spain early in the nineteenth century. The

Ecuadorian historian Jaramillo Alvarado wrote critically, "Not to call 'Republic of Quito' the country which through centuries of its existence was known as Kingdom of Quito, Audiencia and Presidency of Quito, State of Independent Quito, and to call it falsely 'Republic of Ecuador,' was a mistake." As far as he was concerned, *Ecuador* was a name without traditions and without history. *Quito*, on the other hand, came from the pre-Columbian peoples who lived in the Andes long before the Spaniards arrived.

Cotopaxi Volcano was once thought to be the world's tallest active volcano.

One of the Galápagos Islands

The country of Ecuador has a rich history and heritage, dating from one of the oldest known civilizations in South America. It was part of the Inca Empire and, later, a Spanish colony. Its landscape is stunning, with majestic volcanoes rising from the high Andes, just as La Condamine saw them. East of the mountains, Amazon rain forests and river tributaries roll endlessly to the horizon; to the west, Ecuador's Galápagos Islands lie in the Pacific Ocean. In 1835, another famous scientist, Charles Darwin, observed the unique wildlife of those islands. His studies led to the development of his theory of evolution, published in 1859. Ecuador may be one of the smallest countries in South America, but some of the continent's most interesting scientific discoveries originated there.

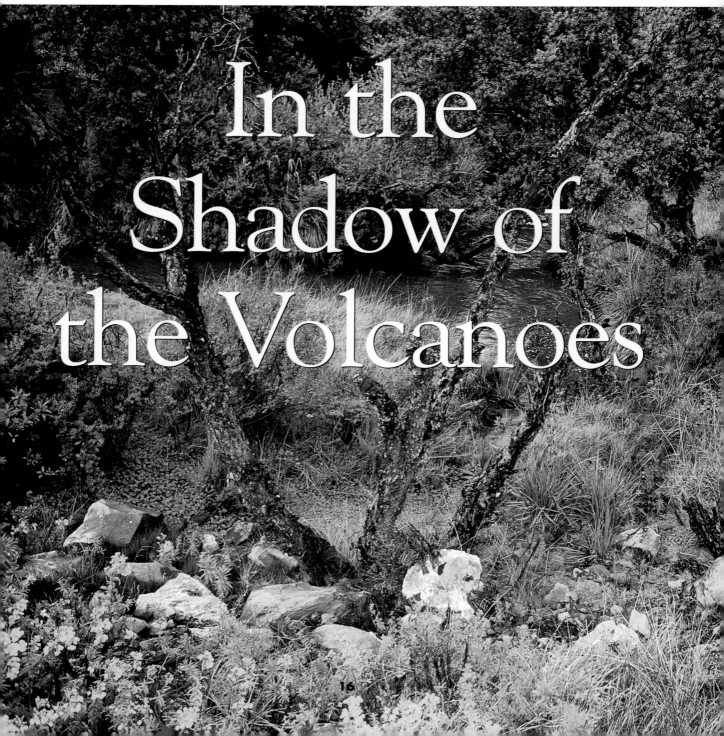

In the Shadow of the Volcanoes

E CUADOR IS THE SMALLEST OF THE SOUTH AMERICAN Andes Mountain republics. To the north, it shares a boundary with Colombia, and to the south and east, it borders Peru. The Pacific Ocean bathes a forested coastline to the west, while east of the mountain ranges, wide rivers drain to Amazonian forests and eventually into the Atlantic Ocean. The Galápagos Islands, famed for their extraordinary wildlife, lie 600 miles (966 km) west on the equatorial line.

The Galápagos, made up of nineteen main islands and numerous islets, are also known as the Archipiélago de Colón. The archipelago is a province of Ecuador. The islands cover a total area of 3,086 square miles (7,992 square kilometers), making up less than 3 percent of the nation's territory.

Ecuador is slightly smaller than the state of California, and it is also subject to frequent tremors and earthquakes. The cause of this seismic activity is similar in each case. The countless tremors are due to the movement of the Earth's tectonic plates. The Cocos and Nazca Plates beneath the Pacific Ocean push against the South American Plate. The process began between 90 million

Opposite: **A stream in the province of Tungurahua**

UNITED STATES

CARIBBEAN PLATE

PACIFIC OCEAN

COCOS PLATE

ECUADOR

SOUTH AMERICAN PLATE

PACIFIC PLATE

NAZCA PLATE

Ecuador and the Pacific Ring of Fire

· Volcanoes, Ring of Fire

—— Tectonic plates

In the Shadow of the Volcanoes **17**

Ecuador's Geographical Features

Area: 103,930 square miles (269,178 sq. km.)

Largest City: Guayaquil

Highest Elevation and Highest Volcano: Mount Chimborazo, 20,561 feet (6,267 m).

Lowest Elevation: Pacific coast, sea level

Longest Navigable River: Napo River, 700 miles (1,127 km) through Ecuador and Peru

Largest Volcano: Tungurahua (Black Giant)

and 60 million years ago, and the plates' movements created the Andes Mountains, often with jolting earthquakes and spectacular volcanic activity. The process is still going on. Ecuador lies on the notorious "ring of fire"—a belt of volcanoes that ring the Pacific Ocean.

Within 32 miles (51 km) of Ecuador's coast, the ocean floor plunges to depths of more than 9,800 feet (2,987 m), and Andean snowcaps rise more than 20,000 feet (6,096 m) above sea level. The mountains rise abruptly on the east and west. Except for the edges of the Andes in the far north and far south of the continent, the mountains are at their narrowest in Ecuador. In one place, less than 70 miles (113 km) separates lowlands on the Pacific side from the Oriente—the Amazon Basin in the east.

Ecuador is a tiny, often unsung, record holder. No other country can boast so many high volcanoes—thirty in all, many of them active. One snowy summit, Chimborazo, is the country's highest peak at 20,561 feet (6,267 m). It is inactive, and just visible from the Pacific coast.

The Ecuadorian Andes are divided into two main ranges, or *cordilleras*. The eastern range is geologically older than the western range, and a long central valley lies between the two. East of the main ranges lies a smaller and lower range.

The Andes Mountains

Looking at Ecuador's Cities

Guayaquil (below) is located on the west bank of the Guayas River at an altitude of 20 feet (6 m). The city was founded in 1535 by Sebastián de Benalcázar. The 1,973,880 people who live in Guayaquil today enjoy weather with an average daily temperature of 80° Fahrenheit (27° Celsius). Rainfall averages 42.7 inches

(108 cm) annually. Landmarks include the Santo Domingo Church, which was completed in 1548, and the Cathedral of San Francisco.

Cuenca stands at an altitude of 8,468 feet (2,581 m) beside the Río Matadero, in the Pucarabamba Valley. Founded in 1557 by Gil Ramírez Davalo, the city is home to 255,028 people today. Landmarks include the Cathedral at Cuenca, La Concepción Convent, Las Carmelitas Descalzas Convent, and the Museum of Abstract Art.

Machala is in the Pacific Coastal Lowlands, 2 miles (3.2 km) from the Gulf of Guayaquil. A distribution center for cacao and coffee, Machala is home to 184,588 people.

Ecuador's central valley, which averages a height of 8,000 feet (2,438 m), has ten basins, or *hoyas*, where major rivers originate. Quito, the capital, stands in one of these hoyas at an altitude of 9,350 feet (2,850 m), flanked by volcanoes. In the valleys, temperatures are seldom extreme, and the land is intensively cultivated. Snow falls at the highest levels, and many peaks are permanently snowcapped. Heavy rains from January to June are followed by a long dry season, when the sky is often cloud-free until December.

The Avenue of Volcanoes

Nineteen major volcanoes stand in a line along the western cordillera, with more than seven of them rising over 15,000 feet

(4,572 m). Among them are Guagua Pichincha, 15,696 feet (4,784 m), which stands immediately west of Quito and is known to have erupted twenty-five times. One eruption covered the capital with 10 inches (25 cm) of ash. At 17,394 feet (5,302 m), the snowy peak of Illiniza dominates the western side of the central valley only 38 miles (61 km) south of Quito. Carihuairazo—

The cone of Cotopaxi Volcano

16,515 feet (5,034 m)—and Chimborazo rise where the eastern and western cordilleras meet between the cities of Ambato and Riobamba.

The eastern cordillera is dominated by twenty volcanoes, including the perfectly cone-shaped Cotopaxi, which rises 19,347 feet (5,897 m) and overlooks the city of Latacunga. At one time, Cotopaxi was thought to be the world's highest active volcano. It has erupted fifty times in the past 250 years, and in 1877, mudslides started by its eruptions traveled 60 miles (96 km).

Other volcanoes in this range include Cayambe, 18,996 feet (5,790 m), which is almost precisely on the equatorial line; Antisana, 18,714 feet (5,704 m); and Tungurahua, 16,684 feet (5,085 m), also known as the Black Giant and, overall, the

Alexander von Humboldt

Alexander von Humboldt, a young scientist from Prussia (now part of Germany), described Ecuador's central valley as "The Avenue of Volcanoes." Humboldt arrived in Quito in 1802 with French botanist Aimé Bonpland. Together, they made some of the most careful scientific studies of volcanoes of their time.

On his third attempt to climb Pichincha, Humboldt took his scientific instruments to the crater's edge. In only thirty-six minutes, he recorded fifteen earthquake shocks. The people of Quito were accustomed to such tremors, but this time they thought that the young scientist was throwing gunpowder into the crater, and they panicked. They had good reason to be alarmed. Only five years earlier, an earthquake triggered a mudslide that took a massive toll in southern Ecuador. It flattened Cajabamba, the original city of Riobamba, and killed thousands of people. Humboldt made the first scientific map of Pichincha. It shows both a lower, extinct cone known as Rucu and the active crater Guagua, which is the name used today by volcanologists—scientists who study volcanoes.

Humboldt was fascinated by the volcanoes that seemed to form an "avenue" along the central valley. He connected the volcanoes, their position, and the

tremors to the formation of the mountains. Later, Humboldt and Bonpland climbed to 18,893 feet (5,759 m) on Chimborazo. They failed to reach the summit only because their route was broken by a 400-foot (122-m)-deep chasm. Even so, their ascent remained a world record for more than thirty years.

Today, Guagua Pichincha is still active and still alarms the citizens of Quito. Like many of the country's volcanoes, Guagua Pichincha is closely monitored by Ecuadorian volcanologists as well as by visiting scientists from around the world.

largest of them all. A spectacular inactive volcano with many small peaks is El Altar, at 17,725 feet (5,402 m). The Spaniards thought it resembled a church and gave the peaks names such as "The Bishop," "The Tabernacle," and "The Canon."

The fiery summit of Sangay—17,159 feet (5,230 m)—is one of the world's most active volcanoes. At night, it often casts a glow on the surrounding forest and showers ash and boulders almost continuously. Another volcano rising from the forests is *El Reventador* (The Exploder), which stands at 11,680 feet (3,560 m). Much of the year, it is hidden in the clouds of Amazonia. Its eruptions—twenty-four in the past 450 years—are often detected by sound, shaking, and smell

The 1995 volcanic eruption on Fernandina Island

alone. The Exploder is so well hidden that its exact geographical position was not known until 1921.

Ecuador's Galápagos Islands are also volcanic. There are fifteen volcanoes in the archipelago's nineteen main islands. None of these mountains is higher than 5,541 feet (1,689 m). The most continuously active is Fernandina (4,904 feet [1,495 m]) on Fernandina Island. In early 1995, its lava flows entered the sea, killing many fish and birds.

The Oriente

Although the volcanoes and the Galápagos Islands often grab the headlines, the lowlands east and west of the mountains make up almost three-quarters of Ecuador. The Oriente, a land of Amazonian rivers and forests east of the Andes, covers approximately half of the country.

Earthquakes

The list of Ecuadorian earthquakes is impressive, and few Andean towns have escaped damage. The 1797 earthquake that devastated the town of Cajabamba also destroyed Latacunga, a small colonial city south of Quito. Only a few miles north of the equator, Otavalo, today a colorful market town, was largely destroyed in 1868. Tulcán, on the border with Colombia, was struck in 1923, and the pretty town of Ambato, south of Quito, suffered considerable damage in 1949.

The same shocks hit Baños, in the eastern ranges, and totally devastated a nearby small town, Pelileo, for the fourth time in 300 years. More recently, in March 1987, an earthquake struck the route of the trans-Andean pipeline carrying oil from the Oriente, causing severe environmental damage. In one spot, a 25-mile (40-km) section of the pipe ruptured, allowing a mixture of oil and mud to flow through the forests into rivers.

Cabins in the Oriente

Before the formation of the Andes, the ancient rocks of the South American continent sloped gently westward, and originally the rivers drained toward the Pacific. Millions of tons of sediment were deposited in what is now the Amazon Basin, covering much of the ancient rock. As the mountains grew, the ancient base tilted slightly in the opposite direction. Today, rivers that begin in the Andes and flow eastward lead eventually to the Amazon and, with it, flow to the Atlantic. The sediments are still there and beneath them lie the fossil fuels of gas and petroleum.

The northernmost Ecuadorian river flowing to the Amazon is the San Miguel River, which forms part of the border with Colombia. This river joins the Putumayo, a much larger river flowing from Colombia that also forms part of the border. The Aguarico and the Coca Rivers start in the snows of Cayambe Volcano on the equator. They make a torrential journey downhill to the Napo River, which runs 700 miles (1,127 km) slightly southeastward to join the Amazon. The Napo rises in the eastern cordillera close to Cotopaxi Volcano. The snows of El Altar and Tungurahua feed the Pastaza River, which flows southeast to the Marañon, a huge Amazon tributary beginning in Peru.

The Coastal Lowlands

West of the Andes, the lowlands are only 112 miles (180 km) across at the widest point. The mountain slopes descend sharply, and the valleys carry rivers to the flatter land below. The major river in the north is the Esmeraldas, draining from the cordilleras just west of Quito. Farther south, around Chimborazo, the rivers drain to the Guayas, the largest river on the west coast. The Guayas empties into the Gulf of Guayaquil, which is studded with low islands. The largest of these is Puna, where the first Spanish explorers stopped on their journey south from Panama to Peru.

A stream running into the Pastaza River

Journey to the Freshwater Sea

A simple sign on an old building in Quito commemorates the first recorded descent of the Amazon River from the Andes to the Atlantic. The mouth of the Amazon was already known and had been named "the freshwater sea," but the journey along its course across South America happened more by luck than by plan.

In December 1540, Francisco de Orellana, a Spaniard, set out from Quito with an expedition in search of El Dorado, a fabled land of great wealth. The party headed east in a blizzard across the eastern cordillera, flanked by the snows of Antisana Volcano. They made a steep descent into the thick, cloud-drenched mountain forests, where they followed tumbling streams and paths never seen before by a European. They were lost for weeks in tangles of plants in a maze of steep valleys where they found little food and were frequently ambushed by local Indians. They passed the San Rafael Falls and eventually reached the wide Coca River.

After six months, they were still only 78 miles (125 km) from Quito. Suddenly the river changed, becoming wider and slower with sandy banks. They had reached the almost level plain of the Amazon Basin. The explorers decided to build a small boat, and on November 11, 1541, they set out with the current, still hoping to find El Dorado. Instead, they came to the Napo River, and by Christmas, they had reached the river we know as the Amazon. There was no turning back, and for another eight adventure-filled months they followed the Amazon to its mouth.

Most of the western lowlands are less than 980 feet (300 m) in altitude. The only higher ground is near the coast between Guayaquil and Esmeraldas. Much of the coastline is forest- or mangrove-fringed and has a humid climate. From December to June, rainfall is high—usually about 40 inches (102 cm)—and flooding is common. There is little temperature variation between seasons.

Only one area, the Santa Elena Peninsula on the northern side of the Gulf of Guayaquil, is truly dry. The low rainfall in this region is due to the cooling and drying effect of the coastal current, which comes from the chilled ocean depths and sweeps north, close to the coast. Near the Santa Elena Peninsula, this current turns westward toward the Galápagos Islands.

Occasionally, the current is disrupted by a warm, south-flowing current known as El Niño, which probably begins far to the west over Tahiti. The name *El Niño* was used originally by South Americans and has now entered global use for its effect on world climate. El Niño can do great damage. For example, the coast of Ecuador was severely hit in 1997–1998, with flooding and landslides in many areas. More than 200 people died, roads and bridges were washed away, crops were destroyed, and the nation's fishing industry suffered huge losses.

Women walking along a highway that was damaged by El Niño in 1998

Símon Bolívar

Bolívar Province stretches from the high grasslands near the snows of Chimborazo down the western slope of the Andes and on through dense rain forests to the lower Cordillera de Guaranda. The province was named for Símon Bolívar (right), the great patriot and liberator of many of Spain's South American colonies. Bolívar was born in Caracas, Venezuela, in 1783 and educated there. After traveling in Europe, he returned to Venezuela in 1807 convinced that the colonies should be independent of Spain. He led Republican forces in Venezuela against the Royalists from 1810 until 1819 with mixed success and was exiled several times. In 1819, he marched his troops from Venezuela on an amazing eleven-month journey across the Andes into Colombia. There, at the Battle of Boyacá on August 7, 1819, Bolívar defeated the Spaniards, and Colombia was free. He won independence for Venezuela at the Battle of Carabobo in June 1821, and his lieutenant Antonio José de Sucre ended Spanish rule in Ecuador a year later. Together, they defeated the Spaniards in Peru and Bolivia in 1824–1825.

Green Gold

FEW PLACES ON EARTH OF A SIMILAR SIZE HAVE THE GREAT variety of plant and animal life found in Ecuador. The country's position astride the equator, its high mountains, and the influence of the Pacific Ocean and the Amazon River have given Ecuador a diversity that staggers the imagination. Many of Ecuador's plants are rich sources of natural medicines and other materials. The genes, or building blocks of life, of such plants are in increasing demand today, and, as genetic research progresses, the plants are worth more than their weight in gold.

To put Ecuador's plant diversity into perspective, an area near the Coca River holds more than 6,000 plant species, many of them unique to that region. A 1987 study revealed more than 25 species of trees never before recorded. By comparison, a rich North American forest may have fewer than 4,500 species, all of which have been studied extensively.

The Coca River site has been designated a Center of Plant Diversity (CPD). It covers an area of approximately 3,475 square miles (9,000 sq km) around Sumaco Volcano (13,090 feet [3,990 m]) flanked by mountain forests rich in species. Sumaco last erupted in 1933. Like most of South America's forested regions, however, this site is constantly threatened by road building and other human activities. Fortunately, one part of this extraordinary land has been established as the Sumaco-Napo-Galeras National Park, and a

Opposite: **A giant tortoise of the Galápagos Islands**

much smaller area is an established biological reserve. Ultimately, it is hoped that the entire area will become the Gran Sumaco Biosphere Reserve, with the protection it deserves.

Yasuni National Park and Waorani Ethnic Reserve

Ecuador has five more CPDs, each carefully selected. A site in the Amazonian region has special importance and is protected as the Yasuni National Park and Waorani (or Huaorani) Ethnic Reserve. Just a few miles east of the point where the Coca and Napo Rivers meet, it is a gently undulating land, with an altitude ranging from 656 to 1,148 feet (200 and 350 m).

National Parks and Reserves

- National Parks
- Reserves

This area has a variety of tropical rain forest plants. Trees with trunks 10 feet (3 m) across reach up to 150 feet (46 m), thrusting their flowering crowns high above the canopy. Tough lianas hang like ropes from the highest branches, and festoons of mosses or bromeliads with luxuriant leafy whorls fill every space. Other parts of the forest are open swampland where anacondas—giant constricting snakes—and other reptiles live.

The entire region is at the level of the Amazon lowlands. In the rainy season when water pours from the mountains, the rivers flood, depositing rich silt on each side of their course.

National Symbols

Ecuadorians have chosen the Quina quina as their national tree. Known to botanists as the *cinchona*, this tree has smallish yellow or pink flowers and reaches a height of 30 to 40 feet (9 to 12 m). Its bark has medicinal properties. Bark extract has long been used by the native Americans of the Andes to fight fevers. Cinchona is in the same family of plants as coffee and the North American partridgeberry.

While the cinchona comes from the forested lower slopes of the Andes, Ecuador's national bird is from higher parts. The Andean condor, the world's largest flying bird, has a wingspan of up to 10 feet (3 m) and weighs 20 to 25 pounds (9 to 11 kilograms). Condors are rare in Ecuador today, but early explorers saw many of them, often feeding on carcasses of sheep or llamas.

As the floods recede, this fertile land, or *varzea*, is exposed. During the dry season, plants grow quickly on the varzea and may cover it entirely if the river changes its route.

Other rivers carry less silt because they rise in the forest itself, where the soil has been leached by rain and only rotting vegetation remains. The Yasuni River is a so-called black river, stained with plant dyes from the decaying forest. Here, where the food chain starts, the animal life is limited. Even so, this is a special habitat for trees that grow in flooded places, including palms.

A collared peccary

This lowland forest has been inhabited by generations of native American people—the Waorani (or Huaorani). Many game animals live here, including deer and various rodents, some as large as small pigs. The forest equivalent of a pig—the peccary—is also found here. It roots between the trees for soft plant shoots, small animals, and fallen fruits. The plant kingdom supplies all the Waorani needs of fruit, nuts, dyes, string, and wood for weapons and building materials. These forest people also have their own natural medicines and poisons. They use plant extracts to treat snakebites and tooth decay, and they use other plants as a local dental anesthetic and to cure fungal skin disease.

A colorful toucan

Birds are numerous in the reserve. In the evening, flocks of parrots screech loudly as they cross the canopy. Macaws and toucans are the most colorful birds; harpy eagles, king vultures, and storks are the largest.

It is no coincidence that this CPD is one of a series of unique places across the extent of Amazonia from the Andes to the Atlantic. In the 1970s, scientists began to realize that some pockets of forest had unusually high percentages of species that were different from those in the surrounding Amazonia. This discovery led to speculation that the species had evolved over tens of thousands of years in isolation, as if they had been on an island. Further research led to the conclusion that during the ice ages of the Pleistocene era, the forest shrank to mere patches—or hot spots—separated from one another by grasslands or muddy plains. These patches of ancient forest—or *refugia*—became centers of plant

The Tiniest Record Holders

Ecuador is a bird-watcher's mecca. Its enormous variations of altitude mean variations in temperatures, rainfall, soils, and plants. These combine to create thousands of habitats occupied by more than 1,500 species of birds. No group of birds exhibits this exuberant variety more than the hummingbirds. The hummingbird family is confined to the Americas, and Ecuador is the center of hummingbird diversity.

These birds are usually small, seldom weighing more than 1 to 2 ounces (28 to 57 grams), and they get their name from the distinctive humming sound made by the rapid beating of their wings. They feed on nectar from flowers and tiny soft insects or arthropods. Perhaps the most remarkable of these tiny birds is the sword-billed hummingbird, whose bill is as long as its head and body together. It has appeared on an Ecuadorian stamp.

and animal evolution. When Amazonia warmed up and great forests covered the land again, the refugia remained recognizable by the distinctive species they now contained.

The Yasuni National Park and Waorani Ethnic Reserve lie within one of these ancient refugia. Studies are not yet complete but the parks probably hold more than 4,000 plant species, many of which will be unique.

In the Fire and Snow

Ecuador has set aside seventeen areas as national parks or reserves. Six of these are in the mountains, and two include spectacular volcanoes. Cotopaxi National Park extends down the eastern slope of the mountain and includes "elfin" forest—reduced in height by cooler conditions—and montane forest.

At higher elevations, extensive open spaces are covered with loose volcanic ash and fine, light rock. It is sometimes possible to see the layers left after volcanic eruptions as bands of color. Near the snowline, Cotopaxi is often cold and windswept. Lichens are one of the few plants that can grow in the highest parts. Other plants form tough, compact groups highly adapted to resist the cold.

Lower down Cotopaxi, hardy grasses conceal the nests of ground doves and a small partridge-like bird—the tinamou. In deep sheltered gullies, the stunted Polylepis tree, a relative of the rose, grows profusely, and tiny frogs hammer an incessant tin-beating sound.

To the south, the constantly active Sangay Volcano, along with El Altar and Tungurahua and much of the surrounding land, has been set aside as another national park and a World Heritage Site. Sangay's crater is virtually inaccessible, and some attempts to climb it have resulted in tragedy. A dense forest covers the base of the volcano, and some of the plants on the eastern side have huge leaves. The protected area extends from an altitude of 2,624 feet (800 m) to the tops of the mountains.

Few mammals live in the higher elevations of this park except for the Andean fox, cavies (wild guinea pigs), and a variety of small rodents. Lower down the slope where the forest begins, mountain tapirs as big as small cows live in bamboo

Below left: **A wild guinea pig**

Below right: **A tapir**

A spectacled bear eating maize

thickets. The forest below is home to spectacled bears, South America's only bear. They live in remote parts of the central and northern Andes Mountains.

The Los Tayos Caves

In the heart of the forest, close to the Coangas River in the southeastern province of Morona-Santiago, is a layer of limestone. It is part of the older, underlying rock of the ancient continent and has been uplifted with the mountains to an altitude of about 1,968 feet (600 m). One of South America's largest cave systems, the Los Tayos Caves, is found here. *Tayo* is the local name for the unusual oilbird, which nests in caves.

The name comes from the fatty chicks, fed by adult birds on oil-bearing palm and other seeds. Native Americans once collected the chicks for their oil.

The Los Tayos Cave system is at least 16,070 feet (4,898 m) long, with passages descending 610 feet (186 m) or more. A scientific expedition in the 1970s found archaeological remains inside one entrance, suggesting its use by early native Americans. The animal life was also fascinating, with many spiders, including the trap-door spider. Scorpions, beetles, and other insects live among the cave-floor debris. Fish and frogs were found in the water, and fruit-eating bats were numerous. Some were carrying wild figs more than half their own body weight. Lancebill hummingbirds nested around the entrance.

Forest Curiosities

The Ecuadorian Andes are clothed with forests at all but the highest levels. Trees once filled the valleys and much of the western lowlands, but this has been changing since Spanish colonial days. The establishment of farms and towns, road building, and other human activities have pushed back forests everywhere.

One special forest has Ecuador's only conifer—the Romerillo, or Podocarpus. It is protected in Podocarpus National Park, situated in the southeast between Loja and Zamora. Conifers, a worldwide group that includes the redwood, are among the oldest survivors on Earth. In Ecuador, Podocarpus trees grow in isolated places. The largest group covers a small mountain range called the Nudo de Sabanilla. This range has a wide variety of altitudes and habitats.

The jaguar is the largest cat in South America.

Balsa trees

Podocarpus National Park is home to more than 500 species of birds, and a group of American and Ecuadorian scientists discovered a new species in 1998. That may not seem extraordinary, but birds have been studied for centuries, and finding something new is a rare event. Among the local mammals are mountain tapir, tiny pudu deer only 15 inches (38 cm) tall, and spectacled bears. Jaguars—the largest of the South American cat family—ocelots, of the same family but smaller, and giant armadillos are found at lower levels.

Ecuador's western lowlands were once covered with lush and virtually impenetrable forests, some scrubland, and mangrove forests along the coast, but much has been destroyed by human activity. One of the most prized trees has been the balsa. Balsa is a light, strong wood. When the first Europeans reached the Gulf of Guayaquil, they found the native American balsa rafts laden with produce, gold, and rare skins.

In the late 1940s, Norwegian explorer Thor Heyerdahl went to Quevedo in western Ecuador to get huge balsa logs to construct his raft *Kon-Tiki*. Heyerdahl started a record-making trans-Pacific journey from Callao, Peru, using the Peru Current to carry him north toward the equator. He knew that the current would then sweep him westward past the Galápagos Islands. Some balsa still grows in Quevedo.

The Enchanted Islands

The Galápagos Islands are one of the world's most famous wildlife sanctuaries. Discovered accidentally in 1535, this uninhabited, desolate volcanic archipelago was described as "enchanted" because the volcanoes seem to rise from a misty ocean. Their name comes from *galápagos*, the old Spanish word for the island's giant land tortoises. The archipelago's unique wildlife arrived there long ago on driftwood floating from the mainland.

The islands were officially adopted by Ecuador in 1832. Three years later, the British naturalist Charles Darwin recorded their unique animals and plants. He was fascinated by the many forms of finch, one of the smaller birds. Darwin discovered finches on many islands, and they were identified as different species. During thousands of generations of isolation, each finch species had apparently adapted to survive in the specific environment of its island habitat. Two species even take cactus spines in their bills and use them to probe for grubs, one of the few known examples of animals using tools. Darwin's scientific writing and that

of another Englishman, Alfred Russel Wallace, who worked in the Amazon, Malaya, and Borneo, paved the way for a new branch of scientific thinking about the evolution of life on Earth.

The centuries of isolation have left the animals of the Galápagos without fear of humans, so visitors can admire them close up, although people are not allowed to touch them. The animal attractions include marine iguanas (left) feeding in the cactus forest, giant 440-pound (200-kg) tortoises wallowing in mud pools, the courtship dance of the blue-footed booby (above), Galápagos penguins, sea lions, fur seals, a few small rodents, bats, and—not least of all—the finches.

Green Gold **39**

Conquest and Independence

HE FIRST PEOPLE TO INHABIT THE ANDES, MORE THAN 10,000 years ago, were nomadic hunters and gatherers. By 3000 B.C., some communities were beginning to settle and produce crops, while others along the coast lived on seafood and fish.

Opposite: **The Inca Sun Temple at Ingapirca**

A ceramic Venus from the Valdivia culture

The Oldest Civilizations

Evidence of very old cultures has been found in Ecuador. The Las Vegas culture, which dates back to about 9000–6000 B.C., lived on the Santa Elena Peninsula. Archaeologists—scientists who study the remains of past human activities—have found Las Vegas shell mounds and posts for thatched houses. In the highlands near Quito, the El Inga site dates to about 9000–8000 B.C. The oldest pottery in the Americas, from about 3500 B.C., comes from the Ecuadorian coast and belongs to a culture known as Valdivia.

The coastal region the Valdivia inhabited is quite remote, and their origins are a mystery because the culture could not have developed in isolation. Some people think there was a Japanese connection; others suggest they were migrant tribes from the Amazon. It seems certain, however, that the Valdivia people traded with coastal tribes as far north as Mexico, and with the coastal, Andean, and Amazonian peoples.

An earlobe ring from the La Tolita culture

Between 500 B.C. and A.D. 1500, several cultures, including the Bahia and the Jama-Coaque, emerged along the coast. The most notable because of its exquisite metalwork was the La Tolita culture. This culture centered on a small island, which experts believe could have been a sacred shrine, off the Esmeraldas coast in the north. Countless pieces of gold and sculptures have been discovered there. La Tolita goldsmiths also worked in copper and in platinum, a metal then unknown in Europe.

Beginning about A.D. 500, the Manteño and the Milagro-Quevedo were the most influential and widespread of these coastal cultures. The Manteño were seafarers who traveled on large balsa-wood rafts with cotton sails. They were also farmers who produced maize, potatoes, manioc, and peppers and raised ducks and guinea pigs.

Many small tribes lived in the highlands, and the most powerful began to emerge by about 1300. These tribes were the Cañaris in the south, the Caras in the region of Quito, and the Puruhuás around what is now Ambato. The Caras and the Puruhuás were governed respectively by the Shyri and Duchicela families, who intermarried to create the greater kingdom of Quitu. The highland tribes were often at war with one another, and relatively little of their culture has survived, mainly due to destruction by the Inca who invaded the region in the fifteenth century.

The Inca

From small beginnings in the Peruvian Andes, the Inca created an empire that included all of Peru and parts of Argentina, Bolivia, and Chile in less than 200 years. About 1460, they marched north into Ecuador but met with fierce resistance from the Cañaris, who held out for several years. The Cañaris were finally defeated in 1472 by Inca Tupac Yupanqui, who then killed most of the male Cañaris. Tupac Yupanqui sealed his success with marriage to a Cañari princess, and their son, Huayna Capac, became the next Inca emperor. The Quitu tribes held out longer, with great ferocity and courage, until Huayna Capac finally conquered them in 1510.

Inca ruler Huayna Capac

When the Inca conquered new territories, they sent uncooperative communities to other parts of the empire where they would not cause trouble. Then groups of loyal Quechua people were brought in to help colonize the new territories. This policy helped to spread the Quechua language—then the common language of the Inca Empire—and allowed officials to keep a close eye on the administration of the conquered lands. In particular, the officials had to ensure they got the *mita*. The mita was a form of tax that required everyone to contribute work or service to the state. An example was building good roads, which the Inca considered vital so that their armies could move quickly to stop any unrest before it got out of hand.

Inca Ruins

After capturing the southern Cañari settlement of Guapondeleg, Tupac Yupanqui began building the city of Tomebamba, which was supposed to equal the Inca capital of Cuzco in splendor and size. But the Spanish conquest put an end to all that, and Ecuador's most important Inca ruin is nearby *Ingapirca* (Inca stone wall), a complex built on the main highway near Cuzco. It was a combination of fortress, temple, and storehouses intended to provide travelers with their every need. Today, the roofless but stout-walled main building overlooks a valley. Around it are intriguingly named ruins such as the Inca's Playground, a large rock with carved channels; the Inca's Face, probably a natural outcrop; and the Inca's Chair, a throne cut into rock. A nearby museum contains some artifacts of the Cañaris and Inca cultures.

Huayna Capac married the daughter of the Duchicela king of Quito, and they had a son, Atahualpa. Sometime between 1525 and 1527, Huayna Capac and many of his court died in a devastating epidemic of malaria or smallpox. It was not clear who his rightful heir was—Atahualpa or his half-brother Huascar, in Cuzco. Huascar probably had the better claim, being of pure Inca blood. Civil war broke out between the two brothers, ending in the defeat and capture of Huascar in a pitched battle outside Cuzco.

Atahualpa

Spanish Conquest

Just as this civil war was ending, a small band of Spanish soldiers led by Francisco Pizarro arrived on the Peruvian coast. Pizarro had visited the Ecuadorian coast some years earlier and now had permission from the Spanish Crown to discover and conquer "Peru."

It was Pizarro's good fortune to find the Inca Empire weakened by civil war. Atahualpa, now the emperor, was based in northern Peru. Pizarro had another stroke of luck when Atahualpa agreed to receive him, believing he was fulfilling an old legend that predicted the arrival of "white men with beards." By deceit and ambush, Pizarro took Atahualpa prisoner, acquired a huge ransom in gold, and subsequently executed the Inca emperor. With just a handful of men, Pizarro went on to capture Cuzco.

The Murder of the Inca Huascar by Order of Atahualpa

PACIFIC
OCEAN

Tacamez — Aug. 1532, Pizarro lands and divides expedition

Quito · Coca

Manta

Ambato

Dec. 1540, Orellana
heads down river

Benalcázar
follows Inca road

Tangaiaia

European Exploration, 1532–1540

▢ Inca Empire 1530	Alvarado 1534
Inca road	Benalcázar 1534
Pizarro 1532	Orellana 1540

**A portrait of
Francisco Pizarro**

In the meantime, Pizarro had instructed his lieutenant Sebastián de Benalcázar to carry the Inca treasure to Panama. But news of the treasure brought the greedy Spanish conquistador Pedro de Alvarado from Central America, intent on taking Quitu. Benalcázar had to act quickly, and he headed north from Peru. An army of Indians led by the Inca general Quisquis blocked his route near the town of Riobamba in Ecuador, but Benalcázar managed to avoid the blockade by taking a detour at night off the main highway. That ended the Inca's last chance to stop the Spaniards.

The Cañaris and Puruhuá Indians were quick to desert the Inca and join the Spaniards. Alvarado was paid off and persuaded to return to Central America, and Benalcázar proceeded to Quitu. When he arrived, he found a city in ruins, burned and deserted by the great Inca general Rumiñahui and his troops. On the site of the ancient town, Benalcázar founded Villa de San Francisco de Quito on December 6, 1534.

Rumiñahui led a counterattack some weeks later, but he was captured and executed. A year later, Benalcázar founded Guayaquil on the coast. The town was destroyed twice by the Indians and built a third time by Francisco de Orellana.

The Spanish Colony

Following the conquest, settlers arrived from Spain, many of them members of the Roman Catholic Church. Priests, missionaries, monks, and nuns took up residence in Quito and other small mountain towns. Many churches, monasteries, and convents were built in Quito, and the Catholic missionaries were largely responsible for opening the first primary schools and universities, bringing in printing presses, publishing the first books, and establishing libraries. By the end of the seventeenth century, Quito's population was about 25,000. Life there and in other highland towns progressed fairly smoothly, helped by the peaceful nature of the local Indians.

In contrast, the port of Guayaquil became an important center for shipping on the west coast, but tropical diseases such as malaria and yellow fever were rampant. The town's wooden buildings were ravaged by insects or destroyed in frequent fires, while the port itself was always in danger of attack from pirates.

Land was divided among the Spanish settlers, including the Jesuit priests. The land was granted on a principle followed throughout the Spanish colonies—the *encomienda*. Under this system, landowners were given a labor force of Indians in return for their efforts to convert the Indians to Christianity. The Indians were treated like slaves and expected to give the landowners a share of their animals and crops. Even the women and children were forced into spinning and weaving.

At the beginning of the eighteenth century, the Spanish settlers took over the remaining areas of land owned by Indians, creating large private farms known as *haciendas*.

Instead of the *encomienda*, the Indians now found themselves forced to work as serfs under the *huasipungo* system, which means "at the door of the house" in the Quichua language. The *huasipungo* system lasted until the late nineteenth century.

Some Indians worked in gold mines in the south, while others were forced to make textiles in sweatshops. The Spaniards introduced European-style looms and sheep to further develop the highly skilled weaving techniques of the Caras and other Indian peoples. Ecuador became the center of the textile trade for all the colonies. The Spaniards also brought in horses, pigs, and cattle and some new crops such as wheat.

Generally, the highland Indians submitted to the Spanish conquerors. Poor working conditions and disease—especially influenza and smallpox, introduced by the Europeans—killed many Indians, but many others survived.

The coastal area was largely neglected during the colonial years because fewer Indians lived there and the region was unhealthy. In the eighteenth century, black slaves were brought from Africa to work on the coastal cacao plantations, and the small mixed population developed a culture very different from that of the highland towns. In the Amazon lowlands, only a few missionaries managed to settle among the Indians, who for the most part remained isolated from the rest of the colony.

For administrative purposes, Quito was made the seat of a Royal Audiencia in 1563, with jurisdiction over what is now Ecuador. Later, Quito became part of both the Viceroyalty of New Castile (now Peru) and the Viceroyalty of New Granada (now Colombia). Except for a tax revolt in 1592, there were few public expressions of discontent against Spanish rule until the second half of the eighteenth century, when the Indians revolted against the Spaniards on several occasions.

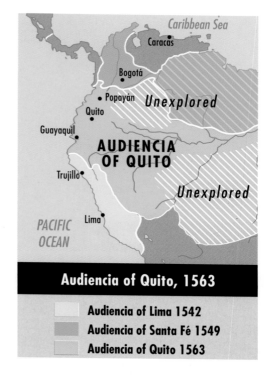

Audiencia of Quito, 1563

Audiencia of Lima 1542
Audiencia of Santa Fé 1549
Audiencia of Quito 1563

Independence

The movement toward independence gathered strength throughout South America during the late eighteenth century, spurred by North American independence, the French Revolution, and the spread of new scientific and political ideas. When Napoléon Bonaparte seized the Spanish Crown in 1809, a small group in Quito were among the first to declare independence from Spain. Their victory lasted only three months before the Royalists regained control and the leaders of the rebellion were killed. Reaction to their brutal deaths led to another rebellion and two years of republican government in Quito before the Royalists again got the upper hand. In 1820, an uprising in Guayaquil ousted the Spanish authorities.

Francisco Eugenio de Santa Cruz y Espejo

Francisco Eugenio de Santa Cruz y Espejo was born in Quito in 1747 to an Indian father and an African mother. In 1767, he qualified as a doctor, but he became a national hero for his stand against Spanish colonialism. He wrote books, and as the editor of the liberal newspaper *Primicias de la Cultura de Quito* was perhaps the first American journalist. Because of his political beliefs, he was jailed, exiled to Bogotá, and eventually died penniless in a damp Quito dungeon at the age of forty-eight in December 1795. Espejo called for complete freedom from Spain, independence for each colony, and the nationalization of the clergy.

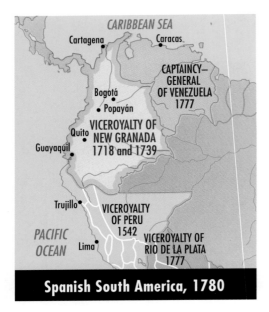

Spanish South America, 1780

A statue commemorating the meeting between Simón Bolívar and José San Martin

People in the highlands had to wait for their freedom until 1822, when the armies of the liberator Simón Bolívar, led by General Antonio José de Sucre, defeated the Royalist forces at the battle of Pichincha.

In 1822, Guayaquil was the scene of the only meeting between two great generals—Simón Bolívar and José San Martin—who had led Argentina and Chile in their battles for independence. They met to discuss the future of Peru and the creation of Gran Colombia. Whatever was said—and no one knows for sure—San Martín went into voluntary exile, leaving the field clear for Bolívar to complete the campaign.

The Audiencia of Quito became part of Gran Colombia in 1821, with Colombia and Venezuela. In 1830, following the breakup of that union, it became the independent Republic of Ecuador.

A Land Divided

Following independence, a struggle for power began between the Conservatives and the Liberals. Generally, the Conservatives were associated with Quito and the people of the highlands, where the aristocracy had retained their large estates, their Indian laborers, and the support of the Catholic Church. The Liberals were centered in Guayaquil, which had become a bustling, cosmopolitan port controlled by a few wealthy, mostly anti-Church merchants. Much of the country's wealth was generated by Guayaquil's industry and trade, and the people there resented paying high taxes to support government officials in Quito. People in Quito, on the other hand, resented having to pay taxes on the goods they were forced to export through Guayaquil. It was the beginning of a rivalry between the two cities that continues to this day.

From 1830 to 1845, the interests of these groups were represented by two military men—Juan José Flores, whose support came from Quito, and Vicente Rocafuerte, backed by Guayaquil. It was essentially a power struggle between two strong personalities, which collapsed when Flores was deposed by the Liberals. Flores had tried to remain in office beyond his term, even inviting the Spanish to come back and support him. The following fifteen years were chaotic as eleven governments came and went. Things were so bad at one point that the mayor of Guayaquil threatened to give his city and southern Ecuador to Peru.

A portrait of Juan José Flores

A Catholic Dictator

Onto this stage walked the extraordinary Gabriel García Moreno, an academic. Having studied his country's problems, he decided that the answer lay in a dictatorship combined with Catholicism. At his request, the Ecuadorian Congress solemnly

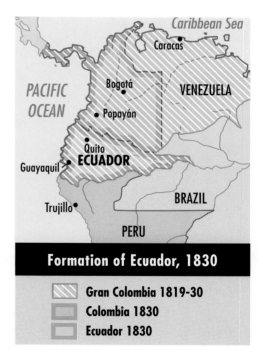

Formation of Ecuador, 1830

Gran Colombia 1819-30
Colombia 1830
Ecuador 1830

Manuela Sáenz

When Simón Bolívar arrived in Ecuador, he had already liberated Venezuela and Colombia from Spain. Everywhere, he was greeted as a hero. Manuela Sáenz first caught his eye as he rode into Quito in triumph, and later they met at a ball. He was thirty-nine; she was just twenty-two and already married to an English doctor. They began a passionate love affair. Whenever and wherever she could, the beautiful Manuela accompanied Bolívar into battle, fighting alongside his troops.

They spent time together in Bogotá, where Manuela saved him from assassination and nursed him back to health. But by 1830, Bolívar was a sick man and disillusioned with his efforts to create Gran Colombia. He decided to go into exile and set off for the coast, leaving Manuela behind. A few months later, he was dead. Manuela was always true to his memory and spent her last years selling cigars in a small coastal town in Peru. She died of diphtheria in 1856.

dedicated the Republic of Ecuador to "The Sacred Heart of Jesus." García Moreno suppressed freedom of speech, censored the press, and banned all opposition while making the Church responsible for all education and welfare and a large amount of government business. Only practicing Catholics could vote, and army regiments were given names such as Guardians of the Virgin and Volunteers of the Cross.

A station on the Guayaquil–Quito railway

García Moreno's measures at least brought fifteen years of peace, and he did many good things for Ecuador. He built roads, schools, and hospitals; began work on the Guayaquil–Quito railway to link the highlands and the coast; and promoted agricultural and environmental reforms. Most of all, he gave Ecuador a sense of national unity. But many people, especially the Liberals, opposed his intolerant religious tyranny. When he tried to have himself reelected for a third time in 1875, he was assassinated on the steps of the Government Palace in Quito.

Rise of the Liberals

The chaotic period that followed García Moreno's death lasted until General Eloy Alfaro became president in 1897. A Liberal, he came from the coast, which increasingly had become linked to the world's markets and international capitalism and had a dominant role in the country's economy. In 1895, Alfaro led a people's army from the coast to Quito, fighting all the way and defeating the government's forces. He was president from 1897 to 1901 and again from 1906 to 1911.

General Eloy Alfaro

Many of Alfaro's reforms were directed at reducing the influence of the Church. Freedom of religion, civil marriage, and divorce were now allowed, and responsibility for education reverted to the state. Alfaro confiscated much of the Church's land, but other wealthy landowners remained powerful, their large haciendas untouched. He completed the Guayaquil–Quito railway.

Alfaro died brutally at the hands of a mob in 1912. The Liberals remained in office, however, and Alfaro was succeeded by General Leonidas Plaza. But real power still lay with the wealthy merchants and bankers of Guayaquil. A short economic boom coincided with World War I (1914–1918), when cacao, rice, and sugar were in demand and the new petroleum industry flourished. Roads, railways, and bridges were built, and towns were modernized.

But it was not enough to avert the depression that followed in the early 1920s, when exports declined and food prices increased, leading to a devaluation of the sucre, Ecuador's money. Workers began to form trade unions, and the level of discontent led to riots in Guayaquil in 1922 in which hundreds of people died. In 1925, the army took control, blaming the country's problems on the merchant bankers of Guayaquil.

If the years since independence had been turbulent, the next twenty-five were the worst Ecuador had ever known. The nation had twenty-two presidents by 1948, when President Galo Plaza was elected. Economic progress, increased agricultural productivity, and foreign exports marked his four years in office, but he was perhaps most proud of having completed his four-year term. He was succeeded by Dr. José María Velasco Ibarra.

President Galo Plaza in 1951

Military Rule

Ecuador had two periods of military rule between 1963 and 1979. The first, which lasted from 1963 to 1966, addressed one of Ecuador's most fundamental problems. Since colonial times,

"The Great Absent One"

Dr. José María Velasco Ibarra earned the nickname "The Great Absent One" for his long periods in exile. He was elected president five times but completed only one term. He was immensely popular with the ordinary people and seemed able to win any election, but his presidencies were marked by erratic and dictatorial actions.

Born into a wealthy family, Velasco Ibarra was educated in Quito and Paris. He first became president in 1934 and tried to break up the large privately owned estates, but Congress opposed him. He was deposed in 1935 and went into exile in Colombia.

Peru's 1941 annexation of a large part of Ecuador's Amazon area led to the downfall of President Arroyo del Rio. By popular demand, Velasco Ibarra was invited to return in 1944 as president. A little more than three years later, he was again deposed, this time by the army. He still had the support of the masses, but he alienated the main political parties. In addition, Ecuador had many economic problems. This time, Velasco Ibarra went to Argentina.

In 1952, after fourteen years in exile, Velasco Ibarra was again elected president, and this time he served his full four-year term. His next presidency began in 1960, but he was removed from office a year

later. Finally, he was elected to his last term in 1968 and, in 1972 he was once more deposed. Again he went into exile in Argentina.

Although Velasco Ibarra dominated Ecuadorian politics for much of the twentieth century, his critics believe he hindered the social and economic development of the country and the traditional political parties. He returned to Ecuador in 1979 to bury his wife and died there a month later.

most of the large estates, or haciendas, had remained in the hands of a few wealthy families, while the majority of the nation's workers were treated like serfs, unable to own the land they worked on. The Agrarian Reform Law introduced in 1964 began breaking up the estates and redistributing the land.

The early years of the second period of military rule, from 1972 to 1979, coincided with a boom in the oil industry. Oil profits were used to fund agricultural, social, and industrial projects and improve the country's transport. This benefited the growing middle classes but did almost nothing to help the poor, who were hit even harder by the severe inflation that followed. In 1979, after seven years of military rule, Ecuador returned to a democratically elected government and produced a new Constitution.

A Troubled Democracy

When Jaime Roldós Aguilera, a young Social Democrat, took office in 1979, he hoped to use oil revenues to increase agricultural and industrial production. He also launched literacy and housing programs. But a drop in oil prices led to an economic slump. In 1981, Roldós was killed in a plane crash and succeeded by his vice president, Osvaldo Hurtado Larrea of the Christian Democratic Party. Hurtado faced a difficult economic situation made worse by the devastating El Niño of late 1982, which destroyed roads, railways, and the banana plantations. Hurtado had to raise taxes and cut government spending, which made his government unpopular.

León Febres Cordero, a right-wing conservative, narrowly won the 1984 elections. He believed in free-market economics, but as oil prices continued to fall, he was unable to curb inflation and stop the recession. The left-wing Congress opposed many of his policies, and there was considerable unrest among the workers and students. Cordero's dismissal of

the armed forces chief of staff, who had accused the defense minister and an army commander of embezzlement, led to a confrontation with the military. In January 1987, Cordero was kidnapped for a few hours, but he was released in exchange for the chief of staff, who was given amnesty.

Economic problems and conflict with Congress continued through the presidency of Rodrigo Borja from 1988 to 1992. He too set out to tackle Ecuador's economic problems, but government-imposed price increases led to mass demonstrations. Anti-government guerrilla groups contributed to the unrest, drug trafficking was another problem, and in 1988 the president of the Supreme Court was assassinated. In 1989, a plot to overthrow the president, led by former president Febres Cordero, was discovered. The following year, an attempt by Congress to impeach President Borja failed.

In 1987, an armored car in Quito fires tear gas at students protesting the high prices of oil and bus fares.

Border Disputes

Since independence, Ecuador has lost territory to its neighbors. In 1904, it conceded lands in the Oriente to Brazil, and in 1916, Colombia took over an area claimed by Quito for decades. But Ecuador's dispute with Peru has been by far the most serious. It came to a head in 1941, when Peru invaded Ecuador and seized the disputed Amazon area—almost half of Ecuador. The Peruvian army met little resistance from the Ecuadorians, who were poorly trained and equipped.

The rest of the world was too involved with World War II (1939–1945) to take much notice, and in the Rio de Janeiro Protocol of 1942, Ecuador relinquished most of its claims. Since then, Ecuador has denounced the protocol on the grounds that it was imposed by force. Peru claims the land never belonged to Ecuador, that it was Peruvian even before Ecuador was a state.

Intermittent clashes between the two countries in the 1980s and 1990s erupted into war again in 1995. The photo above shows anti-Peruvian graffiti. This time,

the area in dispute was a 30-mile (48-km) stretch of frontier in the Cordillera del Cóndor near the headwaters of the Cenepa River. The backers of the Rio de Janeiro Protocol—Brazil, Argentina, Chile, and the United States—arranged a cease-fire after six weeks of fighting, and in August 1998 troops from both sides withdrew from the area. A peace treaty signed on October 26, 1998, brought the long dispute to an end (below).

A student throws a bomb into an armored police car during a riot against economic reforms in 1994.

President Borja was succeeded by Sixto Durán Ballén of the United Republican Party, with conservative Alberto Dahik as vice president. Their plans included the privatization of many government-owned companies, which led to the loss of thousands of jobs. Widespread protest, with bombings and violent demonstrations, led to a general strike in 1993 and more unrest in 1994. In 1995, the country's attention was diverted to an ongoing border dispute with Peru. The situation called for national unity, and the president's popularity ratings soared.

However, a huge corruption scandal led to the impeachment or resignation of some twenty-three government ministers. Vice President Dahik fled the country, and President Durán Ballén barely escaped impeachment. The next president, in 1996, was Abdalá Bucaram. His term lasted barely six months.

Following an interim period with Fabián Alarcón chosen by Congress as president, new presidential elections were held in July 1998. The winner was the mayor of Quito, Jamil Mahuad Witt.

CHAPTER FIVE

Governing
Ecuador

Congress in session

I N ACCORDANCE WITH ECUADOR'S CONSTITUTION OF August 10, 1979, executive power lies with the president and his cabinet. The legislative branch is represented by the National Congress, and the judicial sector is headed by the Supreme Court.

The president and vice president are elected by popular vote for four-year terms. The president is both chief of state and head of government and cannot serve two consecutive terms. The president appoints the cabinet members.

The 121 representatives to the National Congress are also elected by the people. Seventy-nine members of Congress are elected on a national basis and serve for four years, while 42 members are elected on a provincial basis—two members from each of Ecuador's twenty-one provinces—and serve two-year terms.

Opposite: **The Presidential Palace in Quito**

For the 1998 elections, a woman marks her choices for president, vice president, and Congress.

The representatives elect a president and vice president of Congress, which meets for two months a year. During the rest of the year, all legislative business is carried out by thirty-five members of the Congress who serve on five permanent committees.

All literate citizens aged eighteen to sixty-five are required to vote, except people on active military service, who cannot vote. The Constitution also allows illiterate people to vote, but their vote is not required.

Ecuador is divided into 21 provinces, which are subdivided into 193 cantons, 322 urban parishes, and 757 rural parishes.

The National Flag and Emblem

Ecuador's flag has three horizontal stripes. A yellow stripe covers the top half of the flag, with blue and red stripes below. The colors and pattern of the stripes originated with the Republic of Gran Colombia, of which Ecuador was a part until 1830. Ecuador's national emblem, adopted in 1822, features a condor, Chimborazo Volcano, and the first steamboat built in Ecuador.

NATIONAL GOVERNMENT OF ECUADOR

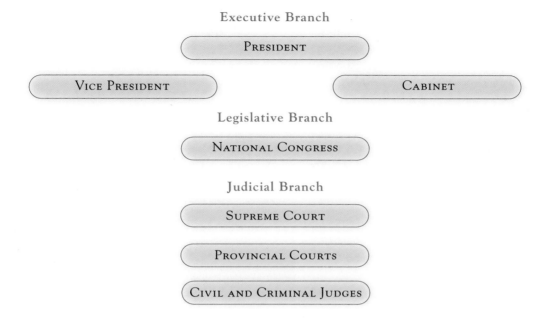

Executive Branch

PRESIDENT

VICE PRESIDENT

CABINET

Legislative Branch

NATIONAL CONGRESS

Judicial Branch

SUPREME COURT

PROVINCIAL COURTS

CIVIL AND CRIMINAL JUDGES

Each province has a governor appointed by the president. All other provincial officials are elected by the people.

There are three levels in Ecuador's judicial system. It is headed by the Supreme Court. The Supreme Court names the members of the provincial courts, who in turn choose civil and criminal judges.

Indian Problems

In May 1990, about 1,000 Indians marched into Quito to demand that President Rodrigo Borja and the government officially recognize the land rights of the Indian peoples. Besides the return of their community-held lands, the group—called the Confederation of Indigenous Peoples—wanted

Quito: Did You Know This?

Quito, Ecuador's capital and cultural center, is located in an Andean valley just south of the equator. It stands at an altitude of 9,350 feet (2,850 m) on the lower slopes of Pichincha, a volcano that last erupted in 1666. In 1534, Sebastián de Benalcázar captured Quito for Spain, and it became the seat of colonial government in 1563. Today, more than 1.4 million people live there.

The average temperature ranges from 59° to 75° Fahrenheit (15° to 24°C) year round, and the city usually gets about 47.5 inches (121 cm) of rain each year. Quito has many churches and convents, including La Compañía (Jesuit), San Francisco, Carmen Alto, San Agustin, Santo Domingo, and the Sagrario.

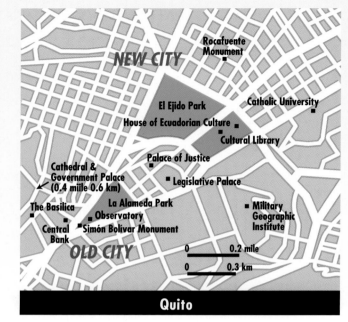

recognition of Quichua as an official language and compensation from petroleum companies for environmental damage in the Amazon. After the Indians seized oil wells in eastern Ecuador, the government agreed to consider the problem and possible compensation.

In 1992, several thousand Amazon Indians descended on Quito with demands for recognition of their homelands. President Borja granted them legal title to a large tract of land in Pastaza Province.

However, there was continuing concern about environmental damage to the rain forest caused by oil companies, and in 1993 a group of Amazon tribes started proceedings against Texaco for compensation of U.S.$1.5 billion. More

Indians and environmental activists rally in front of the state attorney's office in Quito to protest actions by Texaco.

Indian demonstrations broke out in 1994, when the Ecuadorian government prepared to award licenses to other oil companies. In 1995, Texaco agreed to fund some environmental and community projects, but in 1997 a U.S. court rejected the Amazon Indians' claims against the company. The indigenous groups have declared their intention to fight on.

Ecuador Today

In 1998, the devaluation of the sucre, Ecuador's currency, angered the people. They protested against price increases, including an increase of more than 400 percent in the cost of public transportation. The protests continued throughout 1999, with strikes, roadblocks, and protests, until many major

The Bucarams

Asaad Bucaram (above left) and his son Abdalá (above right) have been two of Ecuador's most colorful politicians in recent years. Asaad, whose parents were Lebanese, began work as a textile salesman and was elected to Congress in 1958. He twice became mayor of Guayaquil. A fiery speaker, he got most of his support from the poor of Guayaquil's shanties, but others saw him as a communist. His methods were unconventional. He reputedly used gangs of thugs to get his way and on one occasion brandished a pistol during a debate in Congress. At times he was arrested and exiled, and in 1972 the military prevented him from becoming president when it was clear he was the favorite candidate. He was finally ruled out of the running when the 1979 Constitution stipulated that the parents of presidential candidates must be born in Ecuador. He died two years later.

In 1996, Asaad's son Abdalá Bucaram—self-styled *"El Loco"* ("The Madman")—became president. A former Olympic athlete, he too was popular among the poor. He promised them new housing; higher wages for teachers and health workers; and subsidies for rice, meat, milk, and fuel. But once elected, he failed to keep his promises and seemed determined to live up to his reputation as El Loco, becoming a pop star and regularly appearing on television, singing and dancing. He was removed from office on the grounds of "mental incapacity" and fled to Panama.

groups called for the resignation of President Jamil Mahuad Witt. In a last-ditch attempt to save the economy, Mahaud announced the "dollarization" of the sucre—the U.S. dollar would become Ecuador's currency. This action marked his end. The presidential palace was besieged by thousands of Indians, campesino farmers, students, and workers. The crowds surged around the palace, and Mahuad fled in January 2000, hidden in the back of an ambulance.

For a short time, the presidency was replaced by a non-elected, military-backed committee, but major countries around the world protested the undemocratic system. Loans from international sources were suspended, and for a few days Ecuador was isolated politically and economically. The committee gave in to the pressure, and former vice president Gustavo Noboa was installed as president by Congress.

Noboa supported the dollarization plan even though it was clearly unpopular. Indian leaders said it would benefit only the rich, and the crisis continued. Unfortunately, the answer to the country's woes may not be simple, given the deep gulf between wealthy and poor, especially in Guayaquil, the powerhouse of Ecuador's financial world.

A high-level U.S. mission directed by the Clinton administration met with President Noboa to try and boost the public's confidence in the government. With this U.S. support, the dollarization plan has been almost completely accepted by Congress, and experts believe this is the president's best chance to rescue the nation from its worst socioeconomic crisis in fifty years.

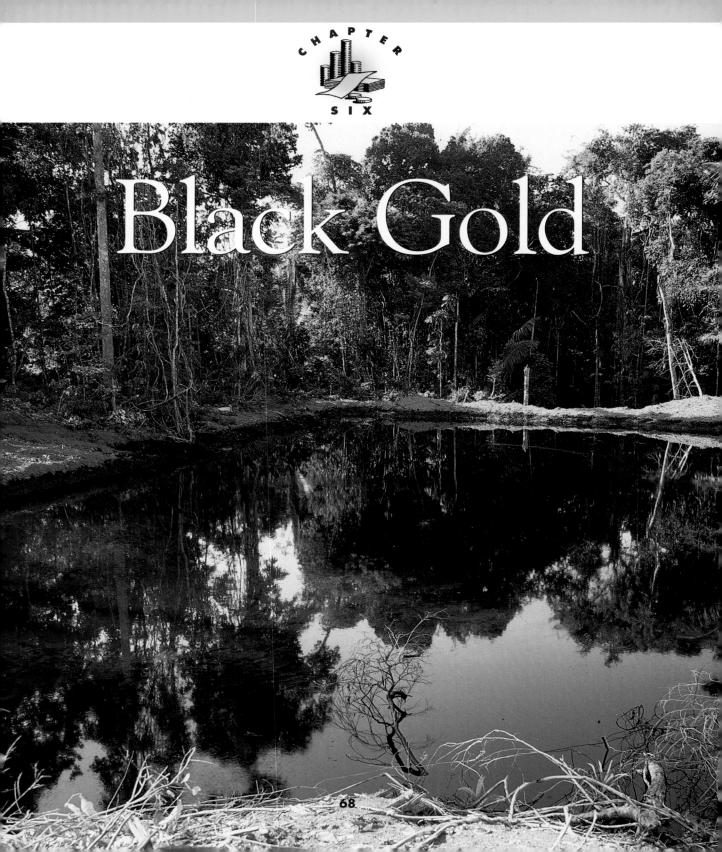

CHAPTER SIX

Black Gold

U NTIL THE MID-1900S, ECUADOR'S ECONOMY WAS primarily agricultural. With the discovery of major oil reserves in the Oriente in the late 1960s, however, the economy became petroleum based. In the 1970s, the government borrowed large sums from international banks and organizations to fund plans for modernization and industrial and social reform. The future profits of the oil industry were used to obtain these loans.

But the world price for oil crashed in the 1980s, El Niño caused great destruction in 1982, an earthquake broke the trans-Andean oil pipeline in 1987, the 1995 war with Peru cost the country a great deal, and in 1997 El Niño brought more devastation. Ecuador was left with huge debts, and today their repayment uses up a large slice of the country's income.

Agriculture

About one-third of Ecuador's workers are involved in agriculture, which produces about 40 percent of the country's export earnings. Ecuador is among the world's leading producers of bananas, and other important cash crops are coffee and cacao.

Opposite: **A pool of oily water near oil well platforms in the Oriente**

Ecuadorians on a plantation wash bananas before packing them for export.

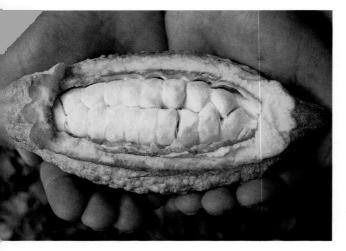

The inside of a cacao pod

The banana plantations, where workers pick, wash, and pack bananas for export, are located along the coast and on the lower western slopes of the mountains. Coffee is cultivated on about one-fifth of all agricultural land, but most coffee farms are small. Cacao was Ecuador's main export for centuries, until a disease known as "witch broom" destroyed many cacao trees in the early 1900s. New trees and fertilizers are being used to increase production. Cacao is grown on plantations and small farms on the coast. Rice and sugar are also coastal crops.

New crops have been introduced to help diversify the economy. These include roses and other flowers, which are cultivated in greenhouses that cover acres of land in the highlands not far from Quito, together with fruits and vegetables, such as strawberries and asparagus. Exports of cut flowers rose from U.S.$5 million in 1985 to U.S.$99 million in 1996.

Flowers being produced for export

Elsewhere in the highlands, women handpick the flowers of the pyrethrum plant for processing into a nontoxic insecticide. Edible vegetable oils are extracted from the African oil palm, which was introduced some years ago, while another relatively new crop—tea—grows well on the eastern slopes of the Andes.

As a result of the 1964 Agrarian Reform Law, there are now many small farms in the sierra that were once part of large estates. By law, each family was given a minimum of 12 acres (5 hectares) of productive land. Today, these farmers grow enough to feed themselves, with perhaps a surplus to sell

Farm fields in the Andes

Women and children gather grains on their farm.

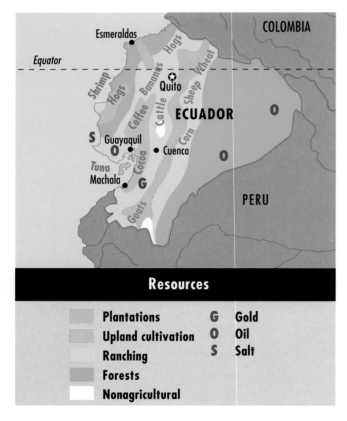

Resources

Plantations	**G** Gold
Upland cultivation	**O** Oil
Ranching	**S** Salt
Forests	
Nonagricultural	

in the local market. Typical crops include potatoes, barley, maize, beans, and other vegetables.

Small farmers cannot easily increase their production. Often, their land is poor and located on steep mountain slopes where the farmers use ox-drawn plows and sow seeds by hand. They need better irrigation, fertilizers, and modern equipment, which few can afford.

Fishing

The shrimp industry in Ecuador is both successful and controversial. In 1995, Ecuador was the world's second-largest shrimp producer. The industry provides employment in areas where previously there was little work, but environmentalists are concerned that development of the coastal shrimp farms has destroyed large areas of mangrove swamps. As a result, the government has set aside a large area in Esmeraldas Province as a reserve.

Other fish catches include sardines, anchovies, whitefish, and tuna, which is exported. Ecuador claims territorial rights 200 miles (322 km) offshore in the Pacific, and has been in dispute with the United States over tuna catches.

A busy fish market in Manta

What Ecuador Grows, Makes, and Mines

Agriculture (1997)

Sugarcane	6,700,000 metric tons
Bananas	5,727,000 metric tons
Rice	1,053,000 metric tons

Manufacturing (1996)

Residual fuel oils	3,215,000 metric tons
Cement	2,930,000 metric tons
Gasoline	1,937,000 metric tons

Mining (1996 unless otherwise noted)

Crude petroleum	19,647,000 metric tons
Limestone	1,900,000 metric tons
Gold-bearing ores (1995)	15,500 kilograms
Natural gas	46,000 metric tons

Oil and Mining

Oil was discovered on the Santa Elena Peninsula, not far from Guayaquil, during World War I. In the 1920s, international companies explored with little success in the Oriente, and it was more than thirty years before large oil deposits were found in its northeastern region. For a short time, the discovery transformed Ecuador's economy, and a pipeline more than 300 miles (483 km) long was built to carry the oil over the Andes and down to Esmeraldas, on the Pacific coast. The industry was largely controlled by Texaco and the Ecuadorian State Petroleum Corporation (CEPE), which bought out Gulf Oil in 1976. Texaco withdrew in 1992.

Following discoveries in the Amazon, Ecuador's known oil reserves dramatically increased in 1993. In the following two years, the Durán Ballén government gave permission for exploration and drilling in the eastern Amazon, which had previously been denied due to protests from the Indian peoples and concern for the environment. Production has continued to increase, and work is underway to expand the capacity of the trans-Andean pipeline. Oil now accounts for about 45 percent of exports and nearly half the government's income.

Gold has been mined in Ecuador for centuries. One of the main centers of gold production is Nambija. Thousands of families live there in harsh conditions, while the miners work in dangerous tunnels that are prone to collapse in torrential rains. Even so, when a new, large discovery was made recently, some 12,000 independent miners rushed to prospect there. Other minerals found in Ecuador include silver, copper, lead, zinc, and cadmium.

The Nambija gold mines in Zamora

The 5,000-Sucre Note

Ecuador's currency is the *sucre*. One sucre contains 100 *centavos*. The reverse side of the 5,000-sucre note shows a giant tortoise and birds from the Galápagos Islands. They symbolize the extraordinary and rare wildlife found only on the islands, which were studied by Charles Darwin and today are Ecuador's main tourist attraction.

Panama Hats

Ecuador's most famous export is the Panama hat. But why is it called a "Panama" hat? The story goes back to the California gold rush in the mid-1800s, when exports from the west coast of South America were transported across the Isthmus of Panama for shipment to North America and Europe. Gold miners traveling from the east coast to the west coast of the United States via Panama were the first to take the hats to North America. They thought the hats were made in Panama, and the name stuck. Panama hats became fashionable in the twentieth century as film stars, political leaders, and other famous people adopted the style. By the 1940s, Panama hat exports represented 20 percent of Ecuador's export revenue.

The hats are made from a fine fiber called *paja toquilla* (toquilla straw). It grows best in Ecuador's coastal lowlands near Guayaquil. The palm fiber is boiled and dried, then taken by truck to weaving villages along the coast. The most famous is Montecristi, where a *superfino*—a top-quality hat—can take up to three months to make. The weaving is often done by women and children with nimble fingers. The hats are then taken to a factory where the loose ends are trimmed and the hats are bleached and shaped. They are then rolled into a cone and wrapped for export.

A Montecristi hat in Europe or North America sells for upwards of U.S.$100, but the weavers earn only a few dollars per hat. It is now hard for them to make a living, and the business is on the decline. Today, only a few families in Montecristi are involved in the Panama hat industry.

Many of Ecuador's factories are in Guayaquil, the main port. About 90 percent of the country's imports and 50 percent of its exports pass through Guayaquil. The largest sector of manufactured goods is connected with agriculture and includes processed foods and drinks, tanneries, and leather goods. The second-largest manufacturing sector includes the oil refineries and petrochemicals derived from the petroleum industry.

Quito has some textile mills that process cotton grown on the coast. North of the city is the thriving town of Otavalo,

Otavaleño women selling handmade wall hangings at the Otavalo market

whose Indian people are famous for their weaving. Tourists visit their weekend markets to buy wall hangings, wool sweaters and scarves, ponchos, and tapestries, but the Otavaleños also run a highly successful textile export business that brings in several million dollars a year. Their products are sold in department stores and specialty shops around the world.

Transport

The Andes, standing between the coast and the Oriente, always made traveling around Ecuador difficult. But the paving of the Pan-American Highway in the second half of the twentieth century transformed the transport system. The highway is the main Ecuadorian road, extending the length of the highlands from Colombia to the Peruvian border. It continues south into Chile and, except for part of Panama, north to the United States.

Within Ecuador, a network of all-weather roads off the Pan-American Highway leads to the coast and to the east. Before the highway was paved, people relied on horses and mules, or they traveled by canoe on the coastal rivers and the Amazon. Today, long-distance buses and trucks reach most parts of the country.

Roads have been part of the plan to open up the Amazon, despite the threat to the Indian people, while airplanes have made some of the most remote parts of the country accessible. Ecuador's railways are slow and unreliable, particularly in the rainy season, when floods and landslides disrupt service.

The Pan-American Highway

Ecuadorians

B EFORE 1964, ECUADORIAN SOCIETY WAS WELL DEFINED. Wealth and power were in the hands of a small, white elite. Most of these people were of pure Spanish descent, and they owned the large haciendas and the best land. Working for them were *mestizos*—mixed-race descendants of Spaniards and Indians—who were managers, stewards, and clerks. They were in charge of the Indians, known as *huasipungueros*, who worked for the landowners as serfs. Relations between the mestizos and Indians were not good. In the coastal lowlands, mestizos were the wealthy merchants and businessmen, while the black and Indian populations remained poor.

Opposite: **A schoolgirl in Guayaquil**

After 1964 and the Agrarian Reform Law, which entitled every Indian to a piece of land, Ecuadorian society began to change. Many Indians remained in rural areas and became independent small farmers. They became known as *campesinos* (country people), a term that now includes rural mestizos. But there was not enough land for everybody, and thousands of people began to drift

Ecuadorians in the town of Quevedo

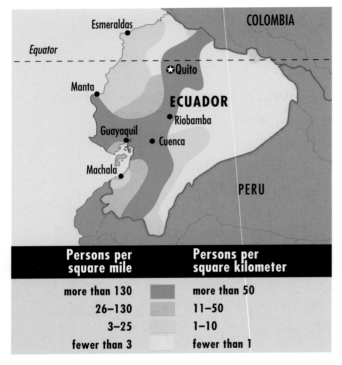

Population distribution in Ecuador

Who Lives in Ecuador?

Mestizo (mixed Indian and Spanish)	55%
Indian	25%
Spanish	10%
Black	10%

toward the towns looking for work. In the late 1960s, the discovery of oil led to a mass migration. Over the next twenty years, about 25 percent of the country's population moved to urban centers in the highlands and lowlands.

The number of mestizos increased with the migration, partly through marriage, but also because many Indians, rejecting their homelands and their traditional dress and speaking Spanish, have assumed a mestizo way of life.

Ecuador today has a population of about 12 million, and more than half of them are considered mestizo. Roughly one-fourth of Ecuadorians are Indian peoples, who live mostly in the Andes. The majority of Ecuador's black population lives in the coastal lowlands. Other minorities include small numbers of whites and Chinese.

Mestizos

Ecuador's middle-class and working-class people are primarily mestizos. Those who are successful business and professional people live much as their affluent counterparts do in the United States or Europe. But this is not the case for most Ecuadorians because the government has been unable to cope with the serious overcrowding in the cities and towns.

Hundreds of thousands of mestizos live in makeshift shantytowns—many without electricity, running water, or permanent housing. In Guayaquil, the shining glass and concrete buildings of the city center stand in stark contrast to the sprawling slum areas on the outskirts.

People came to the towns looking for work, better education, and medical facilities. But fewer than half of Ecuador's workers have full-time jobs. As a result, the city streets are crowded with people trying to make a living by selling everything from champagne to bootlaces or by working part-time as laborers or artisans.

Poor people live in shanties in the Las Peñas district of Guayaquil.

Rural mestizos near Cuenca

Population of Major Cities (1997 est.)	
Guayaquil	1,973,880
Quito	1,487,513
Cuenca	255,028
Machala	184,588

Ecuador's largest indigenous, or native, group is the Quichua, who number between 1.5 million and 2 million. In the Andes, their way of life appears similar to that of rural mestizos. They cultivate maize, potatoes, and beans on small plots of land and make handicrafts for sale in the local markets. Most of them speak Spanish.

But there are differences. As a result of centuries of oppression, the Quichua are submissive and avoid unnecessary

A Quichua village near Zumbahua

contact with white or mestizo society. They distrust outsiders, and although they speak and understand Spanish, they use their own language—Quichua—among themselves. And many *indígenas*, the name they prefer, still wear traditional dress. This applies less to the men than to the women. Many men wear Western shirts and trousers, though they top them off with ponchos. Some men, such as the Cañaris, still wear superbly woven belts with motifs depicting everything from children's toys to traditional Inca designs. The Cañaris weave especially fine ponchos, which they wear for fiestas. The thread used to make them is tie-dyed before it is woven, in a process known as *ikat*.

A Cañari woman wearing characteristic garb

Women's typical dress is a long tunic or skirt with an embroidered blouse, a woven belt, a shawl, and, often, jewelry. Different colors distinguish one village from another, but it is the hat that especially associates a person with a village. These hats come in many styles: large brims, small brims, tall hats, short hats; with and without ribbons; made of felt or straw; trilby-style, round, and all sorts of other shapes.

One of the most unusual forms of dress is that of the Saraguros. They live in the southern highlands near the town of Saraguro. The Saraguros dress mainly in black. They claim descent from Quechua tribes brought to

**A Saraguro man in
traditional clothes**

Ecuador from Peru after the Inca
conquest. According to legend, they
are in eternal mourning for the death
of the Inca emperor Atahualpa.
Saraguro men wear black knee-length
shorts and ponchos, and the women
wear black calf-length pleated skirts
with colored blouses, necklaces of
colored beads, and shawls fastened
with a silver pin called a *topo*. Their
hats have a broad flat brim and are
made of cream-colored, hard felt. The Saraguros make most of
their clothes from sheep or llama wool, which the women spin
by hand and weave in their homes.

A major feature of the indígena way of life is their strong
sense of community. If one family is building a house or needs
repairs done, friends and neighbors are happy to help out and
are rewarded with lots to eat and drink. If there is work to be
done on the village school or on a local road, each family supplies some workers. The same principal works on a personal
level, when couples become *compadres*—a role similar to that
of godparents—to another couple's children. This strong sense
of community and family helps the Andean people to face outside pressures, such as that experienced by the Salasacas near
Ambato. The Salasacas have land that white and mestizo people would like to acquire for agriculture and development.

Unlike the Salasacas, many indígenas work with poor soil
on rocky, volcanic slopes unsuitable for tractors or motor

Languages

Spanish is the official language of Ecuador, but Quichua is spoken by more than 2 million indígenas, or native Indians. It is part of the Quechua language family of Peru and Bolivia, and in Ecuador there are two or three dialects of Quichua. Other native languages belong to linguistic groups including Chibchan and Jivaroan.

The Spanish alphabet has twenty-eight letters. It has no k or w, but includes the letters ch, ll, ñ, and rr. Spanish vowels are always pronounced the same way:

Letter	Pronounce as
a	as in "cat"
e	as in "pet"
i	as in "seek"
o	as in "toe"
u	as in "rude"

Consonants in Spanish are similar to those in English, with some exceptions:

b and v sound alike.

c is like s before e and i.

d within a word is pronounced "th," except after
l and n, when it is like the d in "desk."

ch as in "chair"

h is not pronounced

j has no exact equivalent in English but is similar
to h in "happy"

ll is like y in "yacht"

ñ as in "onion"

qu is like k in "kid"

rr is strongly rolled

vehicles. They use ox-drawn plows, wooden hoes, and digging sticks, and they sow seeds by hand. Most of the small farmers survive on the crops they grow and sell, but some, like the Cañaris, also raise sheep and cattle.

The Saraguros never worked on large estates and were among the first communities to be granted land by the Spanish Crown. They have been independent farmers ever since. Their population now exceeds 20,000, and they have a reputation as cattle breeders and traders. Because their hilly homelands do not provide good pasture, the Saraguros regularly take the cattle to the lowlands to graze, and then return to sell them in the Saraguro market.

Common Ecuadorian Words and Phrases

Following are some common terms and expressions from Ecuador. Several of them—such as those ending in "ay"—show the Quichua influence on Ecuadorian Spanish.

Achachay.	It's cold.
Arrarray.	It's hot.
atatay	disgusting
Ayayay.	It hurts.
chuchaqui	hangover
guambro/guambra	boy/girl (seven years old or more)
huasipichay	housewarming
mushpa	silly
ñaño/ñaña	boy/girl
shunsho	stupid

In addition to working as farmers, many indígenas, especially the Otavaleños, make handicrafts to sell in local markets. Every weekend and some weekdays, the main plazas in Otavalo are full of stalls with an extraordinary array of woven garments, knitted sweaters, wall hangings, blankets, belts, and other items, in addition to vegetables and food of all kinds. The Otavaleños are thought to have inherited their skill from the Caras, who lived in the Quito region at the time of the Spanish conquest.

A display of sweaters handmade by the Otavaleño people

The Otavaleños have traditionally worked in their own homes, even when they were *huasipungueros* on the haciendas. Today, individual families or villages create different items or produce the same items for different markets. One family may make woolen scarves and ponchos, while another makes tapestries. Some sell locally, while others sell their goods in cities throughout South America. About 50,000 Otavaleños work as spinners, weavers, knitters, and salespeople. Their phenomenal success has enabled them to buy back land, acquire new property—including hotels and apartment complexes—and develop other businesses.

Success has not changed their appearance, and their traditional dress is one of the most attractive in Latin America. The men wear dark blue ponchos over spotless white three-quarter-length trousers with a trilby-style hat. The women

An Otavaleño woman and girls in traditional dress

wear similar colors, with long skirts and shawls in wool, cotton—and sometimes velvet—over frilly, white, embroidered blouses. They wear many strands of golden beads around the neck. Both men and women style their long black hair in a single braid and wear cotton sandals. The first language Otavaleños teach their children is Quichua.

Centenarians of the Andes

The tiny village of Vilcabamba in the southern highlands became famous some thirty years ago because many of its inhabitants live well past 100, and anthropologists and other scientists wanted to find out why. Very old people were living a truly active life, walking miles every day to get to their mountainous fields and working from dawn to dusk. But accurate birth-date information was hard to find, and some claims were found to be based on parents' or grandparents' birth certificates. Even so, there had to be some explanation for the high number of very healthy old people. The experts concluded it was physical exercise; a balanced, largely vegetarian diet low in fat; strong family ties; and a relatively calm way of life in an extremely pleasant setting. All pretty much what is prescribed for long life today!

Afro-Ecuadorians

An Afro-Ecuadorian woman from Manta

One community of black Africans settled in the Ecuadorian Andes, in the Chota Valley near the Colombian border. They were slaves who escaped from sugar plantations in Colombia in the middle of the nineteenth century. They lived in isolation in African-style huts of bamboo, mud, and thatch until about 1970. Much has changed since then. The huts have been replaced by brick housing, and the Africans now mix with their mestizo and indígena neighbors, trading and selling in the local markets. Their music, known as *bomba negra*, is a blend of Andean music and African rhythms.

About 1 million blacks or people of black descent live in the coastal lowlands. The first Africans worked as slaves on the cacao and banana plantations. Today, as a result of marriage, the population includes *mulattos*—people of mixed African and European descent—and *montuvios*—people of mixed white, Indian, and black descent, also known as *cholos*.

The slave trade was abolished in 1821, but slavery itself was not ended until 1852. Even then, slaves were tied to their former owners, considered as tenants still owing debt. The debt-tenancy system was abolished in 1881, and the former slaves were finally able to leave the plantations.

Cuaiquers, Cayapas, and Colorados

The only Indian groups to survive in the coastal lowlands are the Cuaiquers (also called the Awa), the Cayapas (also known as the Chachi), and the Colorados, who prefer to be known as the Tsáchilas. Some 1,000 Cuaiquers live on a reserve on the western slopes of the Andes close to the Colombian border. About 5,000 Cayapas live around a river of the same name in the remote northwest corner of Ecuador. They have contact with other coastal peoples but have kept their traditional way of life—growing crops of manioc, cotton, and fruit in the forest and weaving fiber baskets and hammocks for sale. Their bamboo-and-thatch homes are built close to the river on stilts, and they are known to be skilled artisans whose hardwood canoes are traded along the coast. How much longer they can survive in this way is debatable, as speculators are gradually invading their land.

The Colorados take their name from the custom of coloring their hair and painting their bodies with the red achiote plant (right), but today they do this only on special occasions. There are fewer than 2,000 Colorados left, and they live in communities that are part of a reserve near Santo Domingo de los Colorados in the western lowlands.

Today, most blacks hold unskilled jobs. Some work in the fishing industry on shrimp and cargo boats, but many more are employed on banana plantations and cattle ranches. The greatest concentration of Afro-Ecuadorians is in the provinces of Esmeraldas and Manabi.

Minorities

A small percentage of Ecuadorians are of Spanish or other European ancestry or are descended from Lebanese and Chinese immigrants. Most of these minorities live in the cities and larger towns. The Lebanese have been particularly successful business-people in Guayaquil. Quevedo, a small market town in the western lowland, is known as "Chinatown" and its streets are lined with signs bearing Chinese names advertising restaurants, shops, doctors, and dentists. The Chinese originally came to Ecuador to help build the Guayaquil–Quito railway.

Students from Guayaquil

The Galapageños

Patrick Watkins, an Irishman, was the first permanent inhabitant of the Galápagos, when he lived on Floreana Island in 1807. In 1832, an Ecuadorian general established a colony for prisoners and convicts on Charles (Santa María) Island. He was nicknamed "Dog King of Charles Island" because he kept large dogs to control the prisoners.

Floreana was the scene of strange series of events after a German doctor, Friedrick Ritter, and his assistant settled there in 1929. Three years later, they were joined by the Wittner family. Visitors began to come and go, among them a young German woman named Baroness von Wagner de Bosquet. She too decided to settle there, with her two lovers. Soon after her arrival, she began to call herself the Empress of Floreana, a title that was not appreciated by the other inhabitants. Over the next several years, everyone except the Wittner family mysteriously died or disappeared. One of the Wittner daughters, Margaret, lives there to this day.

About 10,000 people now live on the Galápagos, mostly on the islands of San Cristóbal (Chatham) and Santa Cruz (Indefatigable).

People of the Amazon

Six ethnic groups live in the Amazon rain forest. The largest groups are the Quichua, with about 60,000 people, and the Shuar, who number about 30,000. The other groups are tiny by comparison, with no more than 10,000 among them. They are the Achuar, the Huaorani, the Siona-Secoya, and the Cofan. The Amazonian Quichua are almost certainly descended from Quichua people who fled the highlands when the Spaniards arrived. They brought the Quichua language to the lowlands, as well as advanced farming techniques that they adapted to the rain forest environment.

For centuries, the rain forest has provided the indígenas with everything they need: wood and thatch for building their homes; animals and fish for food; cotton for hammocks and the long tunic-like *cushma* that some wear; feathers, seeds, beads, and animal bones for decoration; reeds and palms to

make basketware; hardwoods for canoes, their main form of transport; and medicinal plants to cure illness. The indígenas grow manioc, beans, and fruit in cleared areas of the forest.

At fiesta time, they drink an alcoholic brew made from manioc and play music on flutes, pipes, and drums made from forest wood.

Their way of life changed forever in the twentieth century with the arrival of missionaries, colonizers, settlers, tourists, and the oil and timber industries. Missionaries introduced the concept of money and Western clothing, which most people now wear. The settlers and colonizers have cleared great tracts of forest, especially for cattle ranching. The oil and timber industries have destroyed large areas of forest, built roads, and polluted the air and the rivers, while the tourist companies pay to take visitors to the Indians' homes.

The ethnic peoples are trying to survive and fight back. Some work in the oil industry and on the ranches, while others clear ground for their own pastures and raise cattle. Many earn some money by selling handicrafts to tourist shops, and most groups now receive some form of educational help. But the main issue is their legal right to own the land they have lived on for centuries, and Indian and national organizations are supporting them in this battle. The semi-nomadic Waorani—until recently considered the most primitive group—live in small communities on their large reserve. They have been hit hard by the oil industry and have had confrontations with tourist guides. They have regained some of their land, but the government kept the rights to the oil in their territory. Aware of the money to be made from tourism, the Waorani are making their own deals to promote ecotourism.

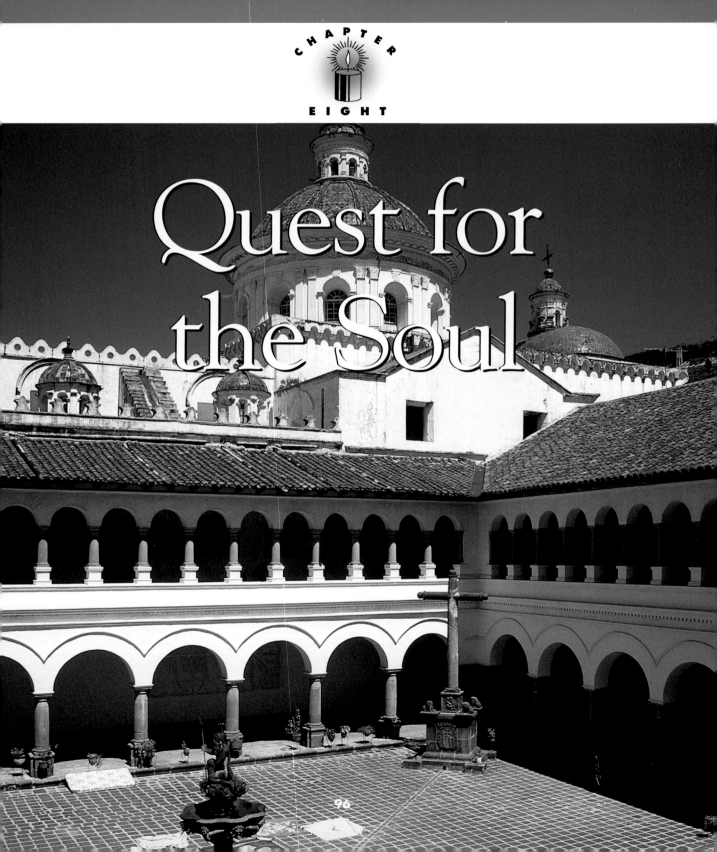

Quest for the Soul

FOUNDED IN 1534 BY SEBASTIÁN DE BENALCÁZAR OF ROMAN Catholic Spain, Quito is the oldest capital city in South America. One estimate suggests that religious buildings, some dating back to the sixteenth century, occupy one-fourth of the old city. In colonial times, the clergy were all-powerful and closely tied to the social elite. The churches were filled as everyone followed a strict routine of daily prayer.

Opposite: **La Merced is a monastery in old Quito.**

Religions of Ecuador

Roman Catholic	95%
Other	5%

Catholicism in Quito

Even today, it is impossible to pass through the old city without seeing some reminder of its connection with the Roman Catholic Church. The morning begins early with bells for the first *misa* (mass), usually attended by the older men and

San Francisco monastery and plaza in Quito

Vendors selling religious articles outside a church

women. Later, other masses are held and some churches are packed with poorer people. The perfume of incense accompanies the ringing of tiny bells. Side chapels are bathed with the light of hundreds of flickering candles, while outside the doors, old men and women sit waiting patiently, their hands outstretched for alms. Rows of stalls are stacked with candles, crosses, aluminum charms, and small pictures of the Virgin Mary and the Crucifixion. Sometimes a wedding or a young girl dressed in white for her first communion draws a small crowd. The religious fervor of the early days is recorded in Quito by South America's finest collection of religious art, including paintings, carved wooden sculpture, and architecture.

But Quito is changing. Piety—once measured in gifts to churches, in numbers of candles burned, or in endless processions and prayer—has given way to commercial life. It is hard to imagine the pace of life here 400 years ago, but in the coolness of the Jesuit Church of La Compañía, the sounds of traffic in the street outside vanish.

Church of La Compañía

The Great Churches

There are eighty-six churches in Quito. The newest, the Basilica, was started in 1926 and is still under construction. San Francisco is the largest and the first church of any size to

The ornate interior art of the Church of San Francisco

The Lily of Quito, Santa Mariana de Jesús

Mariana Paredes y Flores was born in Quito in 1618. Her father was Spanish and her mother was born locally. She was one of eight children in a family of modest means. By the age of twelve, Mariana had decided to become a recluse. She turned her back on the daily life of Quito, with its political and family intrigues, finding peace in the teachings of the Jesuit priests. Her path to sainthood was austere and filled with piety. Her days began with prayers before dawn, followed by confessions and learning in La Compañía.

When she was twenty-six, in 1645, Quito was beset with disasters. Epidemics of measles and diphtheria devastated the population, and earthquakes claimed still more lives. To make matters worse, Pichincha threatened to erupt, and lava began flowing down the slopes. Mariana offered to give her own life to save the city. She went to her room, prayed, and was overcome by an illness. In an attempt to save her life, doctors drew large quantities of her blood, hoping to rid her body of the illness. The blood was poured into the soil at the corner of a courtyard, but the remedy failed.

Mariana died and was buried before the altar of Our Lady of Loreto in La Compañía. Soon afterward, lilies began to grow in the spot where her blood had been poured. They appeared so quickly and at the same time as the scourge of disasters left the city, that it was believed to be a miracle. Mariana's name, lilies, and Quito have been entwined ever since.

be built in South America. This immense church dates from 1553, but in 1868, its twin towers collapsed in an earthquake and had to be rebuilt. The interior is heavily gilded, and many paintings from the sixteenth and seventeenth centuries adorn the walls.

Another great church is La Compañía, famed for its ornate baroque façade and one of its treasures—a painting of *The Virgin Mary*. The painting is framed with emeralds and gold, so it is kept in a bank and brought out only on special feast days. The cathedral was started in the mid-sixteenth century, and the tower and door arch were added 400 years later. Plaques on the outer walls hold the names of the founders of Quito, and the tomb of General Antonio José de Sucre is inside.

Traditional Beliefs

The great churches and many smaller ones in the Andean countryside were not built just for the rich. They were also meant to impress the Indians and to be focal points for religious education. The churches were often built on sites of traditional sacred places, and the Spanish priests were armed with detailed instructions for the eradication of the ancient "pagan" religion. The Catholic priests were dedicated and sometimes ruthless, but they never quite succeeded in their task.

Today's surviving Andean peoples, while nominally Catholic, have kept many elements from the past. Traditional Catholic saints' days were imposed on the sacred days of the

Quichua Indian girls in a Good Friday procession

Bread for the Dead

The celebrating of All Saints' Day and the Day of the Dead on November 1 and 2 is an ancient tradition. People believe that the spirits of the dead return to their loved ones at this time, and families prepare for their coming with special breads and favorite foods. The special breads were originally formed in the shape of small dolls decorated with a simple colored cross, but now there are also donkeys, horses, and other figures. The breads are placed on a homemade altar with other items, including the dead person's favorite food and drink. Once the spirit has visited and feasted, the family heads for the cemetery, where the ceremony is carried out again. It is repeated a year later, and again on the following year, when the family says its final farewell.

Otavaleño Indians celebrate the festival of San Juan.

old calendar, usually coinciding with the movement of the sun. The festival of San Juan on June 24 in Otavalo and Andean villages, for instance, replaces the old Inti Raymi (sun festival) of Inca days.

El Pase del Niño

El Pase del Niño (The Passage of the Child) is a Christmas custom. It commemorates the birth of Christ, *El Niño*. Families all over the country believe it is good luck to have an image of Jesus in their homes, and each year they take it to church to be blessed at a special Mass.

Ecuador's finest celebration of *El Pase del Niño* takes place in the southwestern Andean city of Cuenca. It starts on December 24 with the procession of *El Pase*

del Niño Viajero (The Passage of the Child Traveler), beginning at the Church of San Sebastián and ending at the Church of San Blas. The occasion includes a candlelit vigil beside a crib and music, dances, and a colorful parade in which children and adults decorate cars, donkeys, and horses. This is followed by another procession on January 5 called *El Pase del Niño Rey* (The Passage of the Child King). The festival continues with more passages until Carnival, before Lent.

The Vine of the Soul

The people of Ecuador's Oriente may have been out of touch with the modern world, but they have their own beliefs in life, death, and creation. At one time, it was common for the shamans—or wise men—of a tribe to keep in touch with spirits, both good and evil. To reach out to the unknown, they used hallucinogenic potions made from an extract of a forest vine. While in a trance they chanted, drew pictures, and related stories from the past. Members of the tribe joined in, and festivals were a time for drinking, feasting, and dancing. Except for a few groups still isolated from modern Ecuador, shamans are now simply part of the tourist folklore.

Such festivals are a time for drinking, dancing, and parading in costumes representing local folk legends or themes such as good and evil. The high peaks of the volcanoes are seen as "mountain spirits," and elements of the weather such as lightning and thunder are respected. Mother Earth, or Pachamama, is especially revered in the countryside. Some of these traditional beliefs have found a place in the life of middle-class Ecuadorians and are of increasing interest to visitors from Europe and North America.

New Churches

Although Roman Catholicism is the established religion in Ecuador, its position is being eroded. The politics of the early twentieth century were strongly antichurch, and evangelical groups, including Seventh-Day Adventists and Jehovah's Witnesses, are now bringing their faith to many parts of the country. New churches deliver their message everywhere, even beside the ancient churches of Quito. The Oriente is wide open to evangelism and groups, especially from North America, who are working among people who have had no previous contact with the outside world.

Important Religious Holidays

Epiphany	January 6
Holy Thursday	March–April (varies)
Good Friday	March–April (varies)
Easter Saturday	March–April (varies)
Corpus Christi	May–June (varies)
All Saints' Day	November 1
All Souls' Day	November 2
Christmas Day	December 25

Arts and Crafts

R ICH IN TRADITIONAL HANDICRAFTS, ECUADOR ALSO has a long tradition of fine art—especially religious art, which the Spanish encouraged. Writers have dealt with social and political themes since the nineteenth century. And diverse musical styles reflect the cultures that have found a home here.

Opposite: **Ceramics of the Canelo Indians, a Quichua group who live in the Amazon**

Handicrafts

Panama hats and the weavings of the Otavaleños are Ecuador's most famous handicrafts, but other communities also produce weaving and interesting crafts. The traditional methods of hand-spinning wool and weaving on simple back-strap looms are widespread. With a strap anchored at one end around the woman's waist, and pegged into the ground at the other end, the back-strap loom is easy to move around. Most belts and some ponchos are woven on back-strap looms. Some of the finest belts are made by the Salasacas, especially those dyed with cochineal, a natural dye that comes from insects that live on the opuntia cactus. The Salasacas also make tapestries and blankets on treadle looms.

The Salasaca Indian community's weaving looms

A young sculptor of religious figures in San Antonio de Ibarra

A Canelos Indian woman decorates a ceramic bowl using her own hair as a brush.

San Antonio de Ibarra, north of Otavalo, is a town where almost everyone is involved in wood carving, making items ranging from furniture to religious ornaments. In the same region, Cotacachi is the center of a leather industry producing wallets, bags, purses, and clothing, primarily for tourists. Bags of a different kind come from Cotopaxi province. They are called *shigras*, and are handmade from agave fiber. Originally used to carry foodstuffs, they were said to be so finely woven that they could hold water. Baskets of cane and reed are found in most markets. Gold and silver filigree jewelry is made in Chordeleg, a town near Cuenca.

The Canelos, a Quichua group living in the Amazon, are among the most artistically gifted indígenas. They carve birds and animals from balsa wood, which are then painted and lacquered. While this is a relatively new venture, prompted by tourist demand, their pottery is steeped in tradition. The pots and bowls made by women for domestic and ceremonial use are among the finest found in the Andes today. The best pieces are wafer-thin and decorated with motifs of Canelos life and legend.

Art

The artistic skills of Ecuador's native peoples were recognized early on by the Spaniards, and examples of their decorative wood carvings, sculptures, and paintings are found in many of Quito's churches. Religious themes dominated artistic work through the eighteenth century. After independence, paintings of military heroes and beautiful landscapes reflected national pride.

Joaquín Pinto (1842–1906) was perhaps the first artist to portray the plight of the Indians. He was followed by Camilo Egas (1899–1962); Eduardo Kingman (1913–), who was greatly influenced by the Mexican muralists; and Ecuador's best-known artist, Oswaldo Guayasamín (1919–).

A painting by Oswaldo Guayasamín

All have depicted the Indian people in stylized or abstract ways—sometimes oppressed, often dignified, but generally reflecting their suffering.

La Casa de la Cultura

The Casa de la Cultura is a large, circular glass building in a corner of Quito's El Ejido Park. Inside is the National Museum of the Central Bank, with five adjoining rooms that present the country's history through art. The first two rooms cover Ecuador's pre-Columbian cultures from 4000 B.C. to A.D. 1534, while the last three rooms display paintings from colonial times to the present.

This is Ecuador's finest collection of artifacts, ranging from 5,000-year-old pottery figures of the Valdivia culture to the exquisite gold work of La Tolita. The Valdivia ceramics often represent women, some holding a baby, others pregnant, most with dramatic hairstyles. From other cultures come domestic pots, ceramics of musical instruments, animals, and god figures. The gold work is magnificent, including masks, jewelry, and breastplates. Some cultures worked with

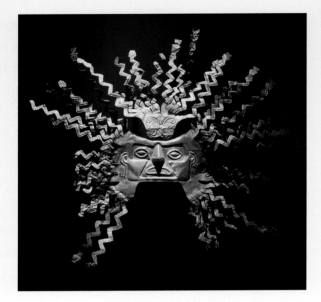

platinum, a metal unknown in Europe until the eighteenth century. The most impressive piece is the golden Mask of the Sun God (above), with radiating beams.

Oswaldo Guayasamín

Oswaldo Guayasamín was born in 1919 in Quito, one of ten children of a mestizo mother and indígena father, a heritage of which he is proud. Following a successful exhibition in 1941 in Quito, his work came to the attention of Nelson Rockfeller, then a major collector of Latin American art in the United States. Rockefeller's patronage enabled Guayasamín to exhibit in the United States. He later moved to Mexico to work with muralist José Clemente Orosco. He also borrowed ideas from expressionism and cubism. His works include murals, paintings, and prints.

Guayasamín depicts the social ills of Ecuadorian society. Many people find his images brutal and harsh, particularly those of indígenas with gaping heads and enormous clutching hands. In 1988, he completed a huge mural of twenty-three panels in the Congress building in Quito, depicting Ecuadorian history. Nineteen of the images are in color; the others, in black and white, represent slavery and dictatorship. In one panel, a skeleton bears the letters C.I.A., for the U.S. Central Intelligence Agency. Despite protests from the U.S. government, Guayasamín refused to blank out the letters.

More recently, Manuel Rendón has at times followed a similar theme, while others such as Enrique Tábara have favored pre-Columbian subjects. Tábara's work includes many pre-Hispanic motifs such as pyramids, snakes, and mirrors. Artist Oswaldo Viteri is a trained anthropologist who uses materials and objects from local Ecuadorian villages, such as the brightly colored little fabric dolls that make up his collage *Eye of the Light*.

Literature

The work of many Ecuadorian writers reflects political and social issues, starting with Francisco Eugenio de Santa Cruz y Espejo in the eighteenth century. Juan Montalvo, a nineteenth-century essayist, wrote at length about social injustice and is famous for his line "My pen has killed him," when he heard of the death of President García Moreno.

The trend continued into the twentieth century, dealing with the gulf between rich and poor, the highlands and the coast, and the plight of the Indians in harsh, realistic language and detail. The most famous and controversial work to emerge from this period was *Huasipungo* by Jorge Icaza (1906–1978). His descriptions of Indian life as brutal, violent, and hopeless angered many people.

Many novelists have come from Guayaquil, including a Guayaquil Group formed by Jose de la Cuadra (1903–1941) and Alfredo Pareja Diezcanseco (1908–). They were joined later by Adalberto Ortiz of Esmeraldas (1914–), who in his novel *Juyungo* relates the life of an Afro-Indian of the region.

Works by contemporary novelists include *Entre Marx y una mujer desnuda* (literally, "Between Marx and a Naked Woman") by Jorge Enrique Adoum, a story based on the author and his friends, and their views on politics, sex, love, and their country. A film based on the book received the Best Director award at the Cuban Film Festival. The city of Cuenca has produced some of Ecuador's best-known poets, including Jorge Carrera Andrade (1903–1978) and César Dávila Andrade. (1919–1967).

The Writing on the Wall

The walls in Quito and many other cities are covered by graffiti. It began to appear in the early 1990s when people—often intellectuals—wanted to express their frustration with social and political conditions. One message, "Forget your dreams, your dreams were sold," summed up the sentiment of many disillusioned people. Many of the graffiti artists belong to permanent groups, usually made up of people from wealthy middle-class backgrounds, who sign off on the walls with their own distinctive signature. Members of the sun-seagull signature group, for instance, are concerned with environmental issues.

Graffiti has become such a significant part of Quito life that the Institute of Culture has published a book with hundreds of examples, and politicians regularly quote the graffiti, if it suits their purpose. "The government is like a local cinema, they get you in and then change the program" is one cynical observation, while another, more humorous, pronounces, "Blessed are the alcoholics, for they shall see God twice."

Ecuador has both traditional Andean music and Spanish, or European, music. Each is performed on distinctly different instruments. Andean music uses wind instruments, drums, rattles, and bells. The wind instruments include the *quena*, a bamboo flute; the *pinkullo*, a smaller flute, and the panpipes, or *rondador*, made of cane and bamboo. The Spanish introduced stringed instruments such as the guitar, violin, and harp.

A relative newcomer is a small guitarlike instrument called a *charango*, usually made with an armadillo shell, which originated in Bolivia. But perhaps the most extraordinary instrument, made by the indígenas after the Spanish introduced cattle, is the *coroneta* or *bocina*—sixteen to twenty cow horns joined together. The accordion and harmonica were

Musicians playing traditional and modern instruments

Men playing marimba music on the beach in Manta

probably introduced in the nineteenth century, and no fiesta would be complete without a thundering brass band. The main dance music in the highlands is the *sanjuanito*, which is played and sung. Men play the instruments and women sing.

The music of the Afro-Ecuadorians on the coast is quite different. Here, the most popular instrument is the marimba, which is similar to a xylophone. Throughout much of the coast, the music combines African rhythm, contemporary *cumbias* from Colombia, and salsas of the Caribbean. But the blacks of Esmeraldas have a purer form of marimba music that alternates impromptu verses between two singers.

Sports

Throughout Latin America, soccer is the most popular sport. There are local, national, and international teams, and although Ecuador itself has not had great success internationally, Ecuadorians avidly follow the fortunes of neighboring Colombia and Brazil. Most towns and villages have *canchas*— small concrete courts—where people play soccer and volleyball, the country's second-most-popular sport.

There are facilities for most organized sports in Ecuador, and tennis has had some notable international success,

particularly by Andrés Gomez. In the 1996 Olympic Games, race-walker Jefferson Pérez won the country's first gold medal, for the 20-kilometer (12-mile) walk. At twenty-two, he was the youngest Olympic champion in the history of the event.

Soccer is the most popular sport in Ecuador.

Andrés Gomez

Andrés Gomez (1960–) is Ecuador's leading tennis player and a star on the international circuit. In 1977, he won the South America Under-18 championship at age seventeen. Two years later, he defeated Vitas Gerulaitis, number three in the world, in the Quito Grand Prix. But he came to world attention when he lost to Jimmy Connors in a U.S. Open third-round match that lasted 4 1/2 hours. Since then, Gomez has had many successes. In 1990, he won the French Open and was ranked number four in the world.

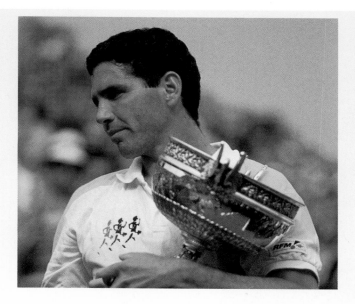

Lifestyles

116

City streets, such as this one in Quito, are always crowded with people and traffic.

THERE IS A MARKED CONTRAST IN THE LIFESTYLES OF PEOPLE living in the various regions of Ecuador. Most of the large cities are in the highlands, and more than 50 percent of the nation's people live in cities. The streets are crowded with people and traffic. People from rural communities regularly come to town to buy and sell in the local markets. All this

Opposite: **An Ecuadorian family in Montecristi**

activity is very different from the laid-back atmosphere of the towns, fishing villages, and banana plantations along the coast. The exception is Guayaquil, a modern, throbbing center of commerce and industry. And the Oriente is yet another world, where the Indian people still live largely in isolation.

The standard of living in Ecuador differs enormously between rich and poor. The relatively small number of wealthy people live in large houses, may own a hacienda, employ servants to run their houses and gardens, and educate

A colonial hacienda and chapel

their children in the best schools. Most middle-class and working-class people live in apartments, in housing complexes in city suburbs, or in makeshift galvanized-iron and wood shanties on the outskirts of the cities. In small towns, adobe houses faced with plaster line the streets, while in rural areas, some houses are still made of adobe mud, brick, and thatch. Houses in coastal regions are usually wooden and may be built on stilts if they are close to a river or swamp.

The family is central to Ecuadorian society, and its female members are closely protected. A woman's role is still largely traditional—marriage in the late teens, with children soon after. But many women work outside the home, and some,

A house made of bamboo and built on stilts

National Holidays in Ecuador

New Year's Day	January 1
Carnival	February–March (varies)
Labor Day	May 1
Battle of Pichincha	May 24
Birth of Simón Bolívar	July 24
Independence Day	August 10
Independence of Guayaquil	October 9
Discovery of America	October 12
Independence of Cuenca	November 3
Foundation of Quito	December 6

such as Doctor Yolanda Kakabadse, who is minister of the environment, have reached the top of their professions.

Health

In 1996, the World Bank noted that more than 12 percent of Ecuadorians were so poor that they could not meet their nutritional requirements even if they spent everything they had on food. Malnutrition continues to be a problem, although international and domestic relief agencies, the Roman Catholic Church, and missionaries provide soup kitchens. The health problem is compounded in poor areas that have no medical clinic, and most people cannot afford medicines.

Two-thirds of Ecuador's doctors and hospitals are in Quito and Guayaquil, where less than one-fourth of the total population lives. The standards of private and state hospitals differ greatly. In state hospitals, shortages of staff and medicines are commonplace. Yet, despite all the difficulties, the standard of health has improved since the 1960s, with a drop in infant mortality and an increase in life expectancy.

Most indígena communities have their own healers, or *curanderos*, who understand the medicinal properties of local plants. They may even use guinea pigs and frogs to help diagnose and cure illness. Illness is often associated with mystical beliefs, curses, and spells, and different kinds of healer–witch doctors deal with these problems. The Shuar and the Taschila are famous for the special healing powers of their *curanderos*.

Herbal medicine for sale at a market stall in Quevedo

Quinine

In 1638, the wife of the viceroy of Peru—the Countess of Chinchón—fell ill with malaria. Legend has it that her physician gave her the powdered bark of the Quina quina tree, and she was immediately cured. The tree was named *cinchona* in honor of the countess. For a time, it was traded by Jesuits and became known as Jesuits' Bark. By the middle of the nineteenth century, the powder was in great demand in tropical parts of the world where malaria was rampant. In particular, the British government needed a supply for its troops in India. Someone, the government decided, must collect seeds from the trees so that they could be sent to India and cultivated there.

That someone turned out to be Richard Spruce, a gentle but determined Englishman who had devoted most of his adult years to the incredible task of cataloging the plants of the Amazon rain forest. In 1860, Spruce organized the collection and packing of some 100,000 well-ripened cinchona seeds and some cuttings. He took them down the Guayas River on a balsa-wood raft for shipment to the Royal Botanic Gardens in London. Eventually, the cuttings flourished into plantations in India—and quina cultivation soon ended in Ecuador.

During World War II, pharmaceutical companies produced synthetic alkaloids to replace natural quinine, but since then some of the organisms in malaria have become resistant to the synthetics. As a result, natural quinine is needed today.

Going to School

Since the 1960s, the government has made real efforts to reduce illiteracy and improve education standards, with some success. Today, about 90 percent of the population can read and write. It has been difficult, however, to make sure that all children go to school.

In theory, children should start school at the age of six, spending six years at primary level and an optional six more— two courses of three years each—at secondary level. In fact, few children complete these courses. Rural areas have fewer schools, and families cannot afford the costs of travel, let alone uniforms and books. Also, children are needed to work, or make what money they can to help the family. Similarly, in poor urban areas, it is a sacrifice for many families to send their children to school.

Opposite: **Secondary schoolgirls in uniform at the San Francisco Plaza**

Central University in Quito

Maintaining good standards in the schools is also a problem due to a lack of funds for training teachers and purchasing equipment. Where there are too few schools, classes are arranged in shifts, usually with primary classes in the morning and secondary in the afternoon. In schools where there are not enough teachers, one teacher may be in charge of all the classes.

Some Indian communities are bucking this trend, though. Otavalo children attend school regularly and complete their courses. Many go on to colleges and universities, and a few attend universities overseas. The Saragueños have their own high school and are among the best-educated indígenas in Ecuador, sending many of their children to universities in Cuenca and Quito. Of further help to indígenas and remote communities are radio broadcasts, including several in the Quichua language. Quichua is still not taught in schools, however, although it is the language of most indígenas.

National Games

Pelota nacional (national ball), a very old Ecuadorian game, is in danger of dying out. It is mostly played by older people. Two groups stand in rows, each holding a board with big rubber studs that they use like a racket to hit a small ball back and forth while a middle group of players tries to stop it.

Much more popular today is a version of volleyball called Ecua-volley. The game fields two teams of three players each. The rules are basically the same as conventional volleyball, though players are allowed to almost catch the ball before returning it. Ecua-volley teams compete in national championships.

Caring for the Children

A large number of children—perhaps as many as 500,000—between the ages of ten and seventeen work on city streets in Ecuador. Mostly, they sell trinkets, cigarettes, sweets, or flowers, or they run errands, clean cars, or shine shoes. Some girls become prostitutes. Ecuadorians are well aware of the problem, and Ecuador was one of the first nations to sign the United Nations 1990 Convention of Children's Rights.

Boys waiting to shine shoes on a sidewalk in Quito

But finding solutions is not easy, and it often falls to the Catholic Church, missionaries, or people of goodwill to help. Ecuador's Central Bank gives support to the *Programa del Muchacho Trabajador* (Working Child Project), one of the best-known programs. Every day, several thousand children in Quito and other towns

Promoting Handicrafts

Olga Fisch arrived in Ecuador from Hungary as a refugee from World War II. She had trained in Germany as an artist and designer, and recognized the quality and potential of the handicrafts made by the Indians. She saw them as works of art and has worked for more than fifty years to promote them both in Ecuador and around the world. She has created a successful company—Folklore—that produces rugs, tapestries, textiles, jewelry, and clothing based on her interpretations of ancient motifs and textile patterns. Some of her rugs are displayed in the United Nations Building in New York City.

are taken to special centers where they get some schooling, are given something to eat, and have the opportunity to play with their friends.

Food

Ceviche is a popular dish in Ecuador.

For most Ecuadorians, the basic foods are rice, potatoes, and cassava—a starchy tuber—with fish or meat and a wide variety of fruit. Some fruits are familiar, such as bananas, pineapples, oranges, and avocados, and others are less well known, such as sweet custard apples and passion fruit. Fish is popular in coastal areas and in the Oriente. Favorite fish dishes are *ceviche*, which is raw fish marinated in lemons or limes and served with onions and chili peppers, and *corvina*, similar to cod, which is fried or grilled. Other fish include squid, shrimps, mackerel, and snapper. Large catfish found in rivers in the Oriente are used to make soups.

Soups are some of the most popular and nutritious dishes in the sierra and include many vegetables combined with pieces of pork, chicken, or beef. Many soups are more like stews. *Sancocho*, for example, is made with green plantains and corn, while *mazamorra* is a thick soup of ground corn, with cabbage, potatoes, onions, and spices. Corn is another popular food, often eaten on the cob. Potatoes, which tend to come with everything, are also cooked as potato cakes with cheese.

Native to the Andes are some nutritious grains such as quinoa, which is usually served in soup but can be eaten like rice. This has been a basic food of the indígenas for centuries. Another traditional dish among indígenas is guinea pig, or *cuy*, which is considered a great delicacy. Indígenas keep guinea pigs in their homes for eating at fiestas. Today, however, wealthier indígenas have begun to buy Western foods such as pasta, sweets, and carbonated drinks, and a growing number of U.S.-style fast-food restaurants are seen in towns and cities.

A Traditional Soup

Fanesca, traditionally eaten at Easter, is an incredibly rich soup. It is made of twelve ingredients: onions, squash, broad beans, *chochos* (similar to beans), corn, beans, peas, *melloco* (a highland tuber), lentils, peanuts, dried cod, and rice. Coming from the highlands and the lowlands, the ingredients symbolize the union of the country, and they are also said to represent the twelve apostles. The origins of the dish are not clear. Some believe it goes back to the days of Jesus, when Christians had to live in hiding. When they left their hiding places, they collected as much food as they could and mixed it all together in a soup.

Timeline

Ecuadorian History

Native cultures flourish.	9000 B.C.–A.D. 1500
The Cañaris, Caras, and Puruhuás tribes gain power; the Cañaris and Puruhuás create the greater kingdom of Quitu.	A.D. 1300–1400
The Inca expand their empire into Ecuador.	1460
The Cañaris are defeated by Inca Tupac Yupanqui.	1472
The Inca, united under Huayna Capac, conquer the Quitu tribes.	1510
Huayna Capac dies; his sons, Huascar and Atahualpa, go to war with each other.	ca. 1526
Atahualpa defeats and captures Huascar; a Spanish expedition led by Francisco Pizarro arrives.	1532
Spain conquers most of Central and South America.	1532–1700
Quito is made a seat of the Royal Audiencia, with jurisdiction over the area now known as Ecuador.	1563
Spanish rule is ousted for two years.	1809
Spanish rule in Guayaquil is overthrown.	1820

World History

2500 B.C.	Egyptians build the Pyramids and Sphinx in Giza.
563 B.C.	Buddha is born in India.
A.D. 313	The Roman emperor Constantine recognizes Christianity.
610	The prophet Muhammad begins preaching a new religion called Islam.
1054	The Eastern (Orthodox) and Western (Roman) Churches break apart.
1066	William the Conqueror defeats the English in the Battle of Hastings.
1095	Pope Urban II proclaims the First Crusade.
1215	King John seals the Magna Carta.
1300s	The Renaissance begins in Italy.
1347	The Black Death sweeps through Europe.
1453	Ottoman Turks capture Constantinople, conquering the Byzantine Empire.
1492	Columbus arrives in North America.
1500s	The Reformation leads to the birth of Protestantism.
1776	The Declaration of Independence is signed.
1789	The French Revolution begins.

Ecuadorian History

The Audiencia of Quito joins Venezuela and Colombia in a confederacy known as Gran Colombia.	**1821**
Ecuador becomes independent.	**1830**
Ecuador endures a series of revolts and dictatorships under eleven presidents.	**1845–1860**
President Gabriel García Moreno establishes strong authoritarian rule until his assassination.	**1860–1875**
General Eloy Alfaro leads a people's army, overthrowing the government.	**1895**
Economic depression hits.	**Early 1920s**
The army seizes control of the government; twenty-two presidents are elected.	**1925–1948**
Peru seizes disputed Amazon land.	**1941**
Ecuador's economy thrives; three elected presidents complete their terms.	**1948–1960**
Economic recession; foreign countries begin developing oil resources in the Amazon.	**1960s**
A military regime takes power.	**1963–1966**
A second military regime seizes power; oil profits are used to fund agricultural, social, and industrial projects.	**1972–1979**
Ecuador democratically elects a president and drafts a new Constitution.	**1979**
Ecuador faces a severe economic crisis.	**1980–1984**
The collapse of world oil prices reduces Ecuador's export revenues by half.	**1986–1987**
Oil export prices increase and government spending is reduced, but inflation rises sharply.	**1988–1992**
Indian groups demand official recognition of their land rights and compensation from oil companies for environmental damage.	**1990**
President Sixto Durán Ballén attempts to privatize many state-owned companies; violent protests and a general strike follow.	**1993**
Ecuador has skirmishes with Peru over the border region claimed by both countries.	**1995**
Ecuador experiences a severe economic crisis; Ecuador and Peru sign a peace treaty.	**1998**
The government is near bankruptcy; people protest President Jamil Mahuad's austerity program with massive strikes.	**1999**

World History

1865	The American Civil War ends.
1914	World War I breaks out.
1917	The Bolshevik Revolution brings Communism to Russia.
1929	Worldwide economic depression begins.
1939	World War II begins, following the German invasion of Poland.
1957	The Vietnam War starts.
1989	The Berlin Wall is torn down, as Communism crumbles in Eastern Europe.
1996	Bill Clinton is reelected U.S. president.

Fast Facts

Official name: *República del Ecuador* (Republic of Ecuador)

Capital: Quito

Quito

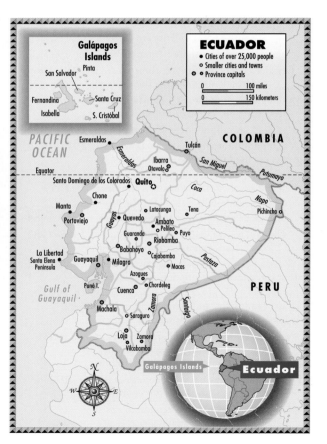

Ecuadorian flag

The Pastaza River

Official language:	Spanish
Official religion:	None
Year of founding:	1830 (seceded from Gran Colombia)
National anthem:	*"Salve, O Patria"* ("Hail, O Fatherland")
Government:	Multiparty republic
Chief of state:	President
Head of government:	President
Area and dimensions:	103,930 square miles (269,178 sq km)
Latitude and longitude of geographic center:	2° 00' South, 77° 30' West
Land and water borders:	Colombia to the north, Peru to the east and the south, and the Pacific Ocean to the west.
Highest elevation:	Mount Chimborazo, 20,561 feet (6,267 m)
Lowest elevation:	Pacific coast, sea level
Average temperatures:	Quito: 59°–75°F (15°–24°C); Guayaquil: 80°F (27°C)
Average annual rainfall:	Quito: 47.5 inches (121 cm); Guayaquil: 42.7 inches (108 cm)
National population (1998 est.):	12,175,000

Population of largest cities (1997 est.):

Guayaquil	1,973,880
Quito	1,487,513
Cuenca	255,028
Machala	184,588

Otavalo weavings

Currency

Students from Guayaquil

Famous landmarks:
- ▶ *Mitad del Mundo* (Middle of the World) monument (Quito), marking the equator
- ▶ *The many churches of Quito*, including San Francisco and the Church of La Compañia
- ▶ *La Casa de la Cultura* (Quito), including the National Museum of the Central Bank
- ▶ *The Otavalo market*

Industry: Petroleum, food processing, textiles, metal work, paper products, wood products, chemicals, plastics, fishing, and lumber

Currency: The *sucre*; in early 2000, U.S.$1 = 25,000 sucres

System of weights and measures: Metric system

Literacy (1995 est.): 90.1% percent

Common Ecuadorian words and phrases:

alpargatas	cotton sandals
Achachay.	It's cold.
Arrarray.	It's hot.
artesanias	handicrafts
campesino	country person
curandero	healer
hacienda	large farm
huasipichay	housewarming
indígenas	indigenous people
ñaño/ñaña	brother/sister
pelota nacional	national ballgame
shigras	bags made from fiber of the agave plant
sanjuanito	a popular dance
superfino	top-quality Panama hat

Andrés Gomez

Famous people:

Jorge Carrera Andrade *Poet*	(1903–1978)
Andrés Gomez *Tennis player*	(1960–)
Oswaldo Guayasamín *Artist*	(1919–)
Jorge Icaza *Dramatist and novelist*	(1906–1978)
Juan Montalvo *Political writer*	(1832–1889)
Jefferson Pérez *Olympic athlete*	(1974–)

To Find Out More

Nonfiction

▶ Beirne, Barbara. *The Children of the Ecuadorean Highlands*. The World's Children. Minneapolis: Carolrhoda Books, 1996.

▶ Davies, David. *The Centenarians of the Andes*. London: Barrie & Jenkins, 1975.

▶ Foley, Erin L. *Ecuador*. Cultures of the World. Tarrytown, N.Y.: Benchmark Books, 1995.

▶ Kendall, Sarita. *Ecuador*. Major World Nations. Broomall, Penn.: Chelsea House, 1998.

▶ Lerner Geography Department. *Ecuador in Pictures*. Visual Geography Series. Minneapolis: Lerner Publications, 1987.

▶ Lourie, Peter. *Lost Treasure of the Inca*. Honesdale, Penn.: Boyds Mills, 1999.

▶ Roos, Wilma, and Omer van Renterghem. *Ecuador in Focus*. New York: Interlink Books, 1997.

▶ Von Hagen, Victor. *South America Called Them: Explorations of the Great Naturalists*. Boston: Little, Brown, 1955.

Websites

▶ **Ecuador**
http://www.ecuador.org/
General information, art and culture, current issues and news, and more from the Embassy of Ecuador; in English and Spanish.

▶ **The Galápagos**
www.wwf.org/galapagos
A World Wildlife Federation site on the Galápagos Islands and the conservation challenges they face; includes a slide show.

▶ **Volcano World**
http://volcano.und.nodak.edu/vw.html
Information on volcanoes around the world, including Ecuador, searchable by region, country, and volcano. Includes satellite images, virtual field trips, interviews with volcanologists, and more.

▶ **Warriors of the Amazon**
http://www.pbs.org/wgbh/nova/shaman/shaman.html
A PBS documentary by NOVA Online on the Huaorani tribe of Ecuador's Oriente region.

Organizations and Embassies

▶ **Embassy of Ecuador**
2535 15th Street, N.W.
Washington, DC 20009
(202) 234-7200
http://www.ecuador.org/

Index

Page numbers in *italics* indicate illustrations.

Meet the Author

"MY FIRST VISIT TO ECUADOR WAS SOON AFTER MY student days in the 1960s. The Quito I saw then was a small, compact city of little more than a quarter-million people. Guayaquil, where I landed from a ship, was a city of a half-million. I was lucky to make several return trips with my husband, and we traveled north and south through the Andes on several occasions, often camping close to the volcanoes. Once, near Chimborazo, a horseman stopped to see if we needed any help, and we talked about his home, the country nearby, and his family. It led to a fascination with Ecuador I have found hard to put down.

"It was twenty years before I managed to return to that same spot at the base of Chimborazo. The road was still unpaved. The tiny thatched field houses were still there, and

so were the people herding their sheep. My friend had gone, but on the surface there was little change. An hour or two later I was in Guayaquil, now a city of 1.5 million with huge bridges, modern roads, and an unnerving pace of life. My work has given me the chance to see the changes throughout Latin America so I was not too surprised, but that day brought home to me just how much this tiny, richly endowed country is one of great contrasts."

Photo Credits